This Book belongs to :

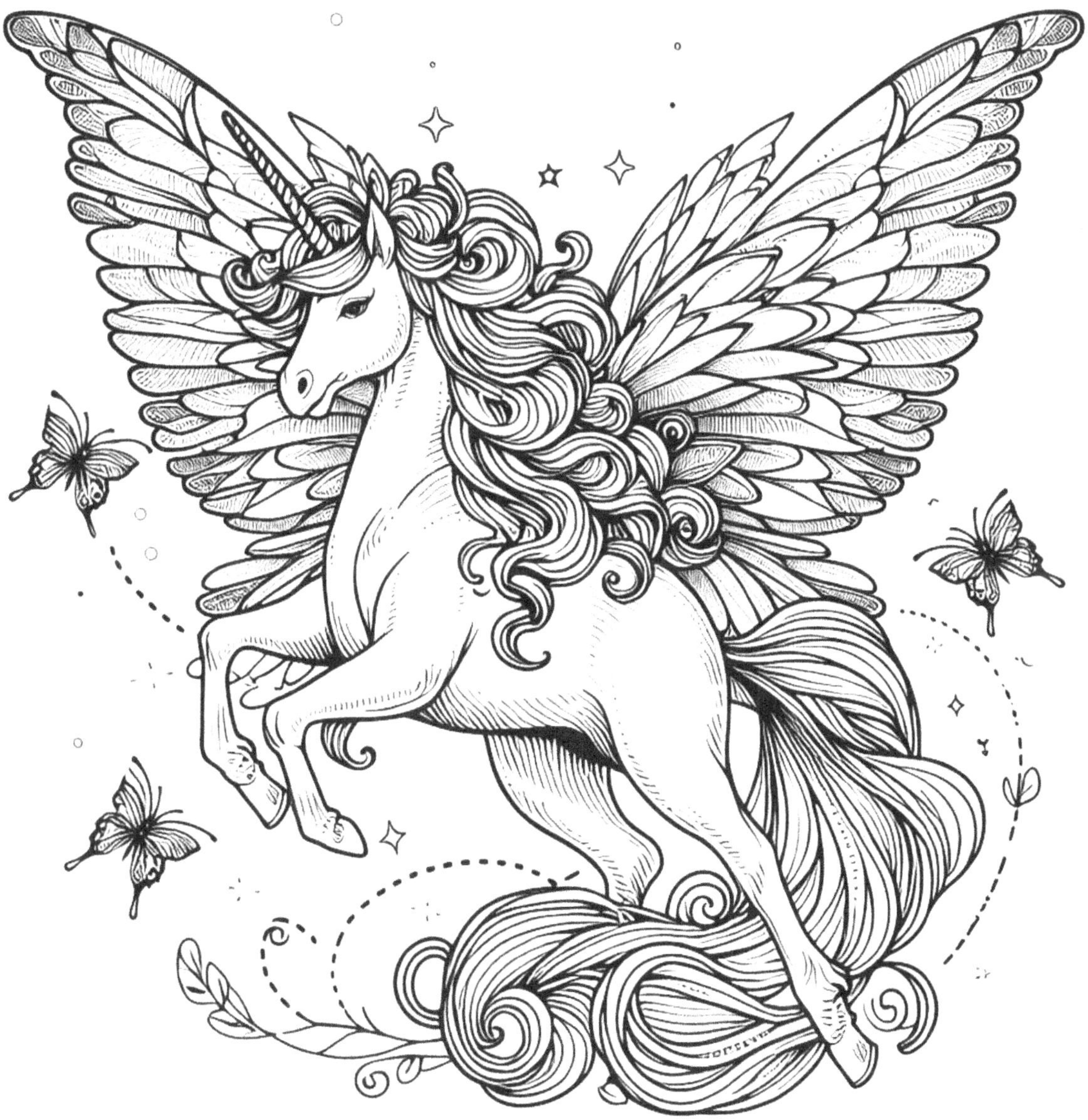

_____

A World of Gratitude

Dear reader,

From the bottom of my heart, I thank you for choosing to embark on this magical journey alongside enchanted unicorns. Each page you color not only brings this fantasy world to life but also brightens my day with joy. I hope that every moment you spend with this book is as special to you as it was for me in creating it.

With love and gratitude, D&E Books

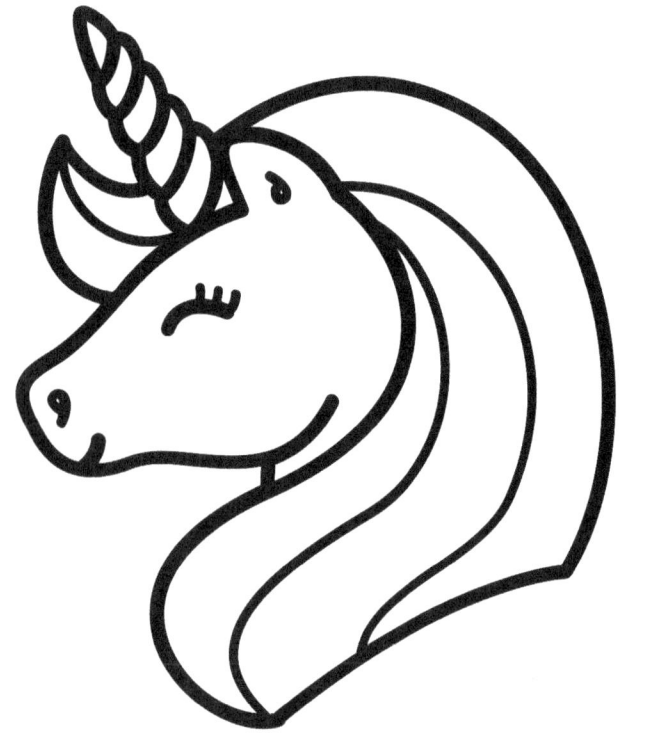

All Rights reserved©

No part of this publications may be reproduced, distributed, or transmitted in any form or by any means, including photocopying, recording, or other eletronic or mechanical methods, without the prior written permission of the publisher, except for brief quotations incorporated in critical reviews and other specific noncommercial uses.
Any unauthorized replica of this book is prohibited.

Test Color Page

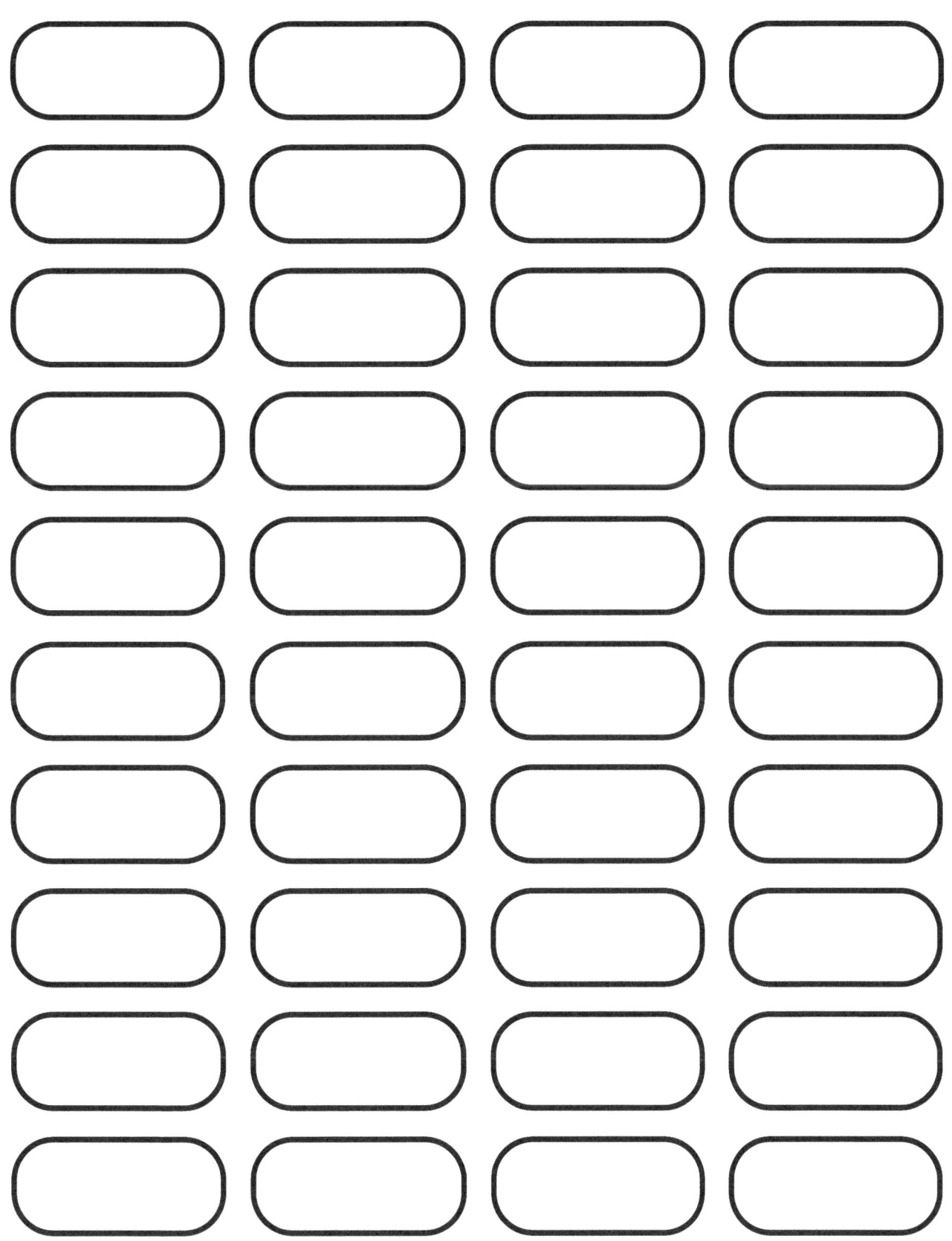

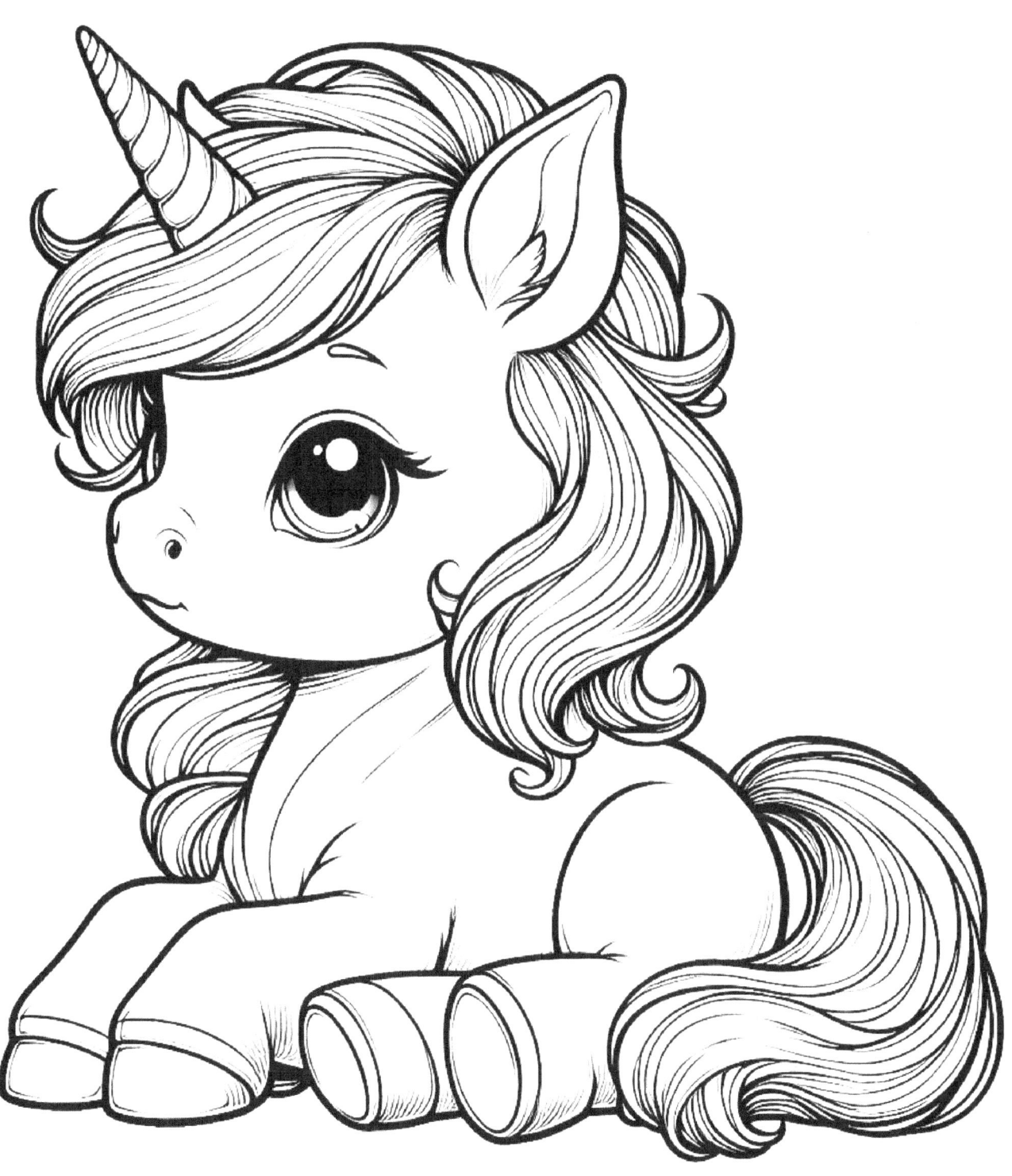

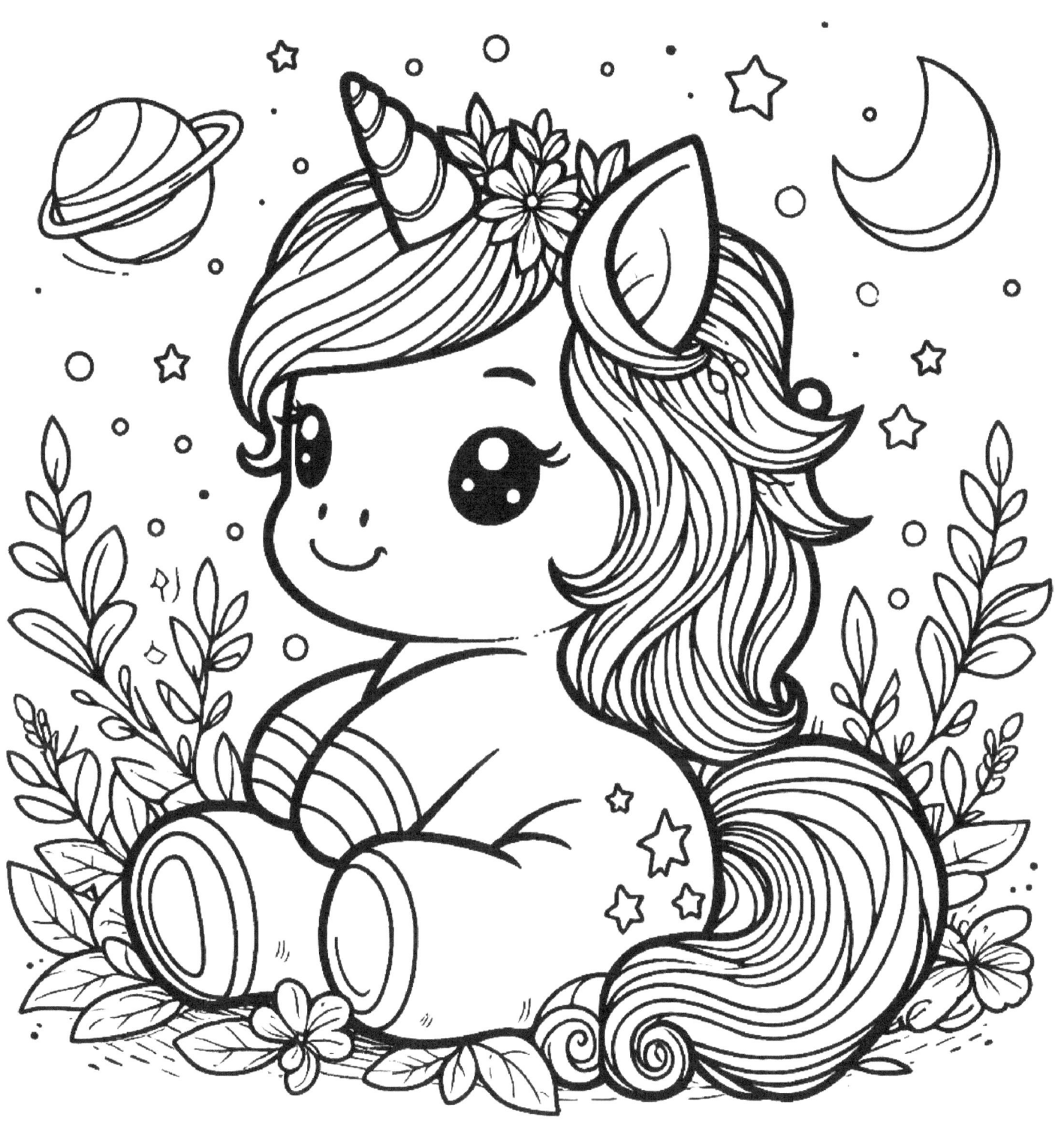

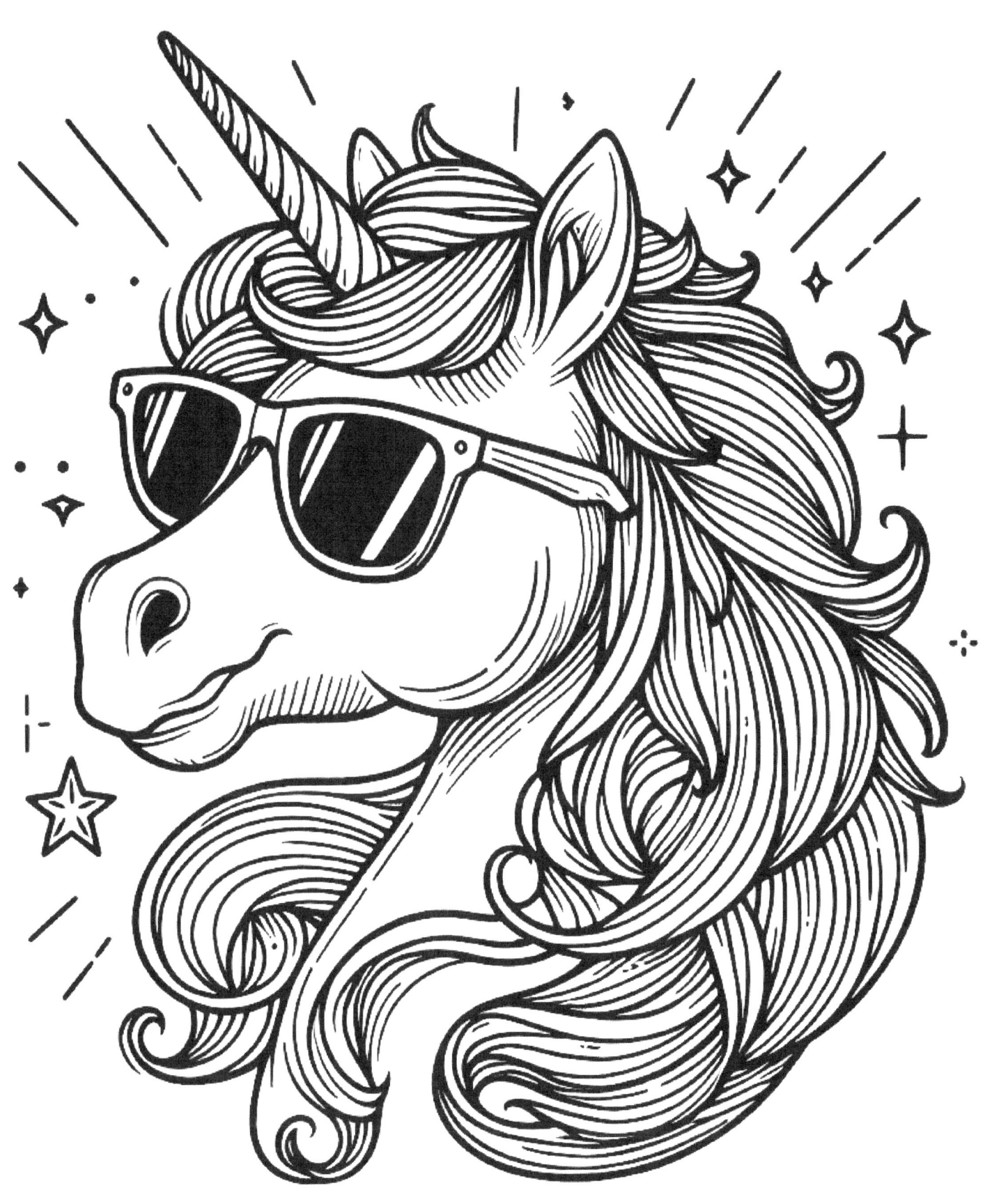

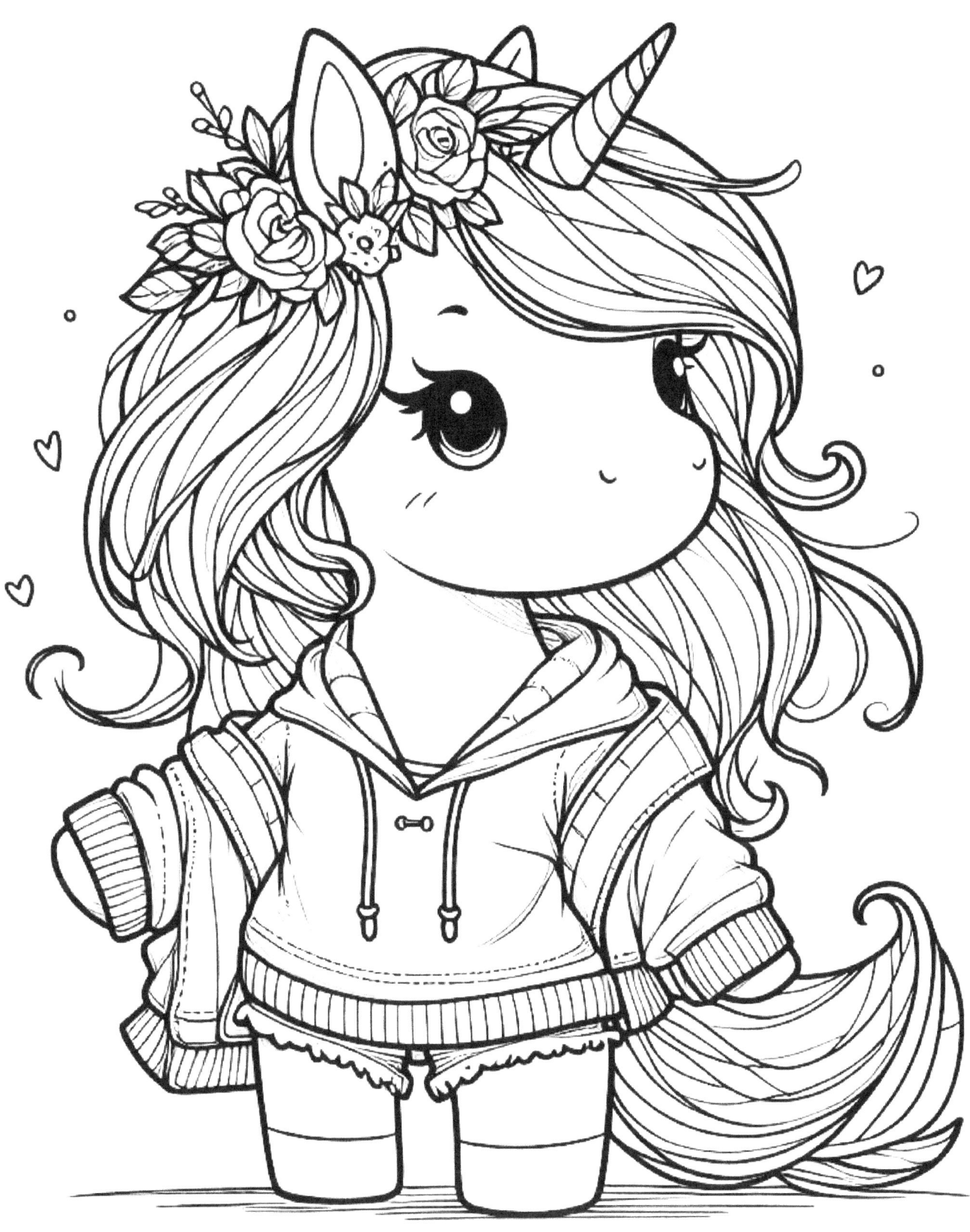

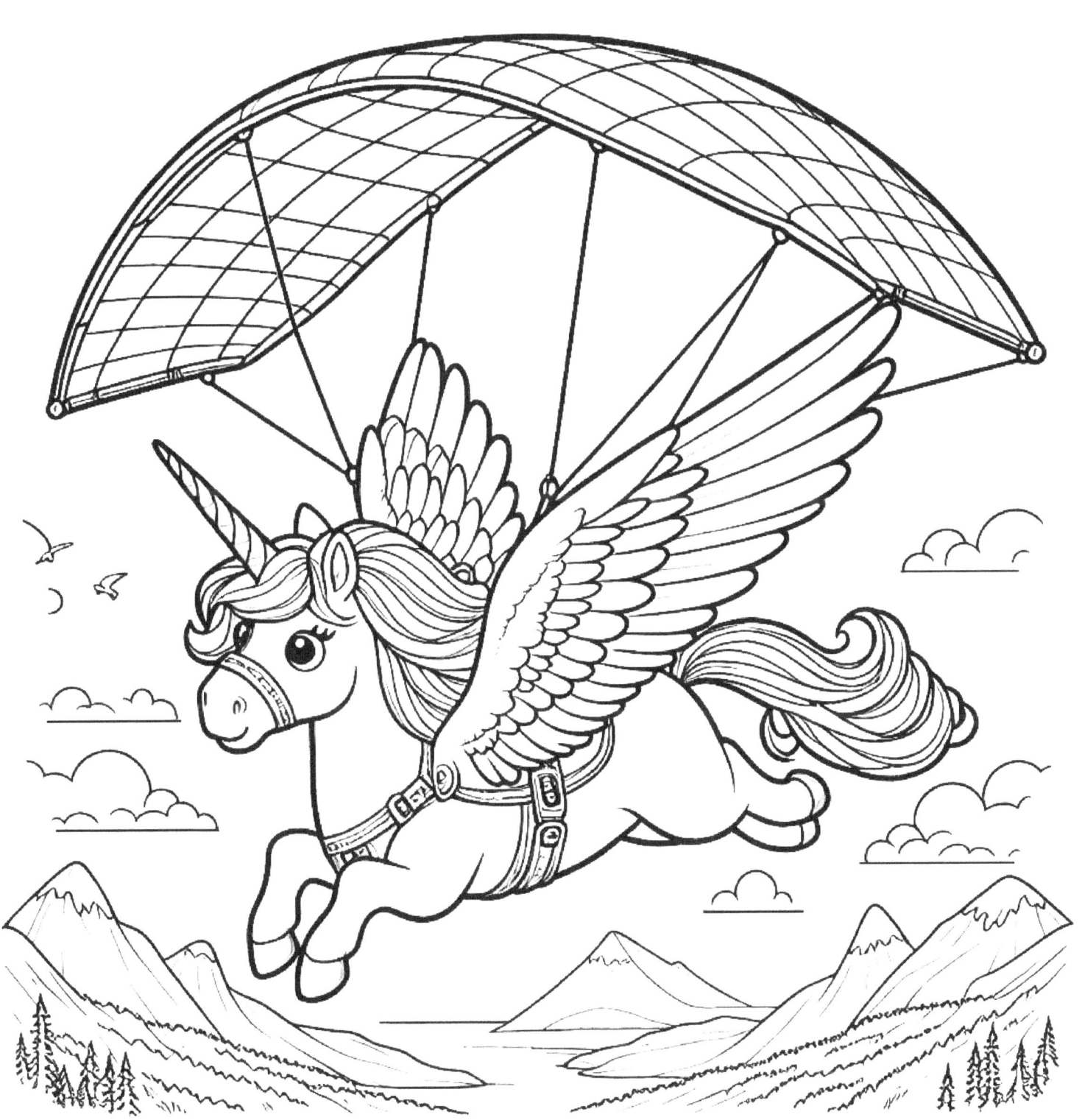

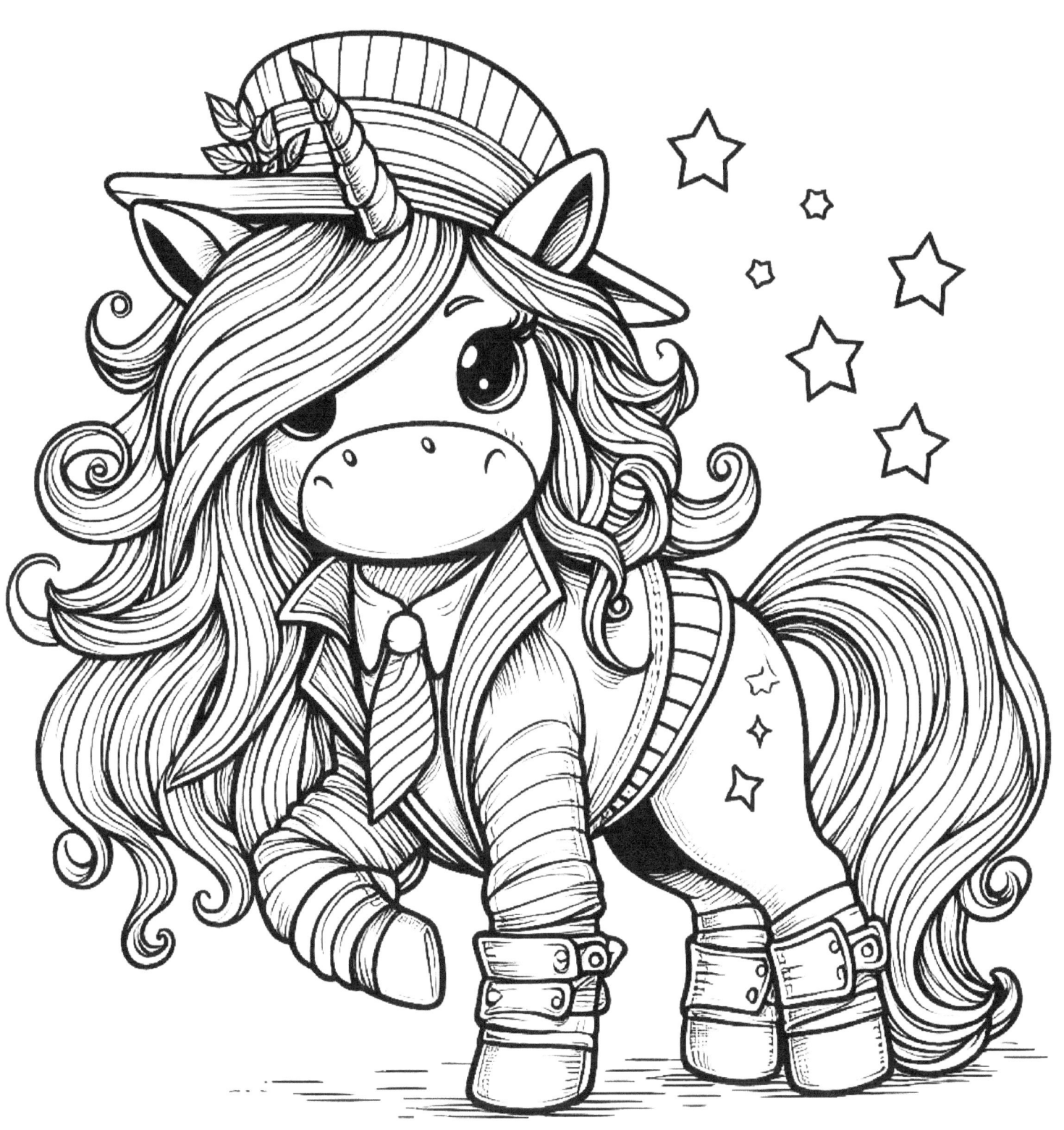

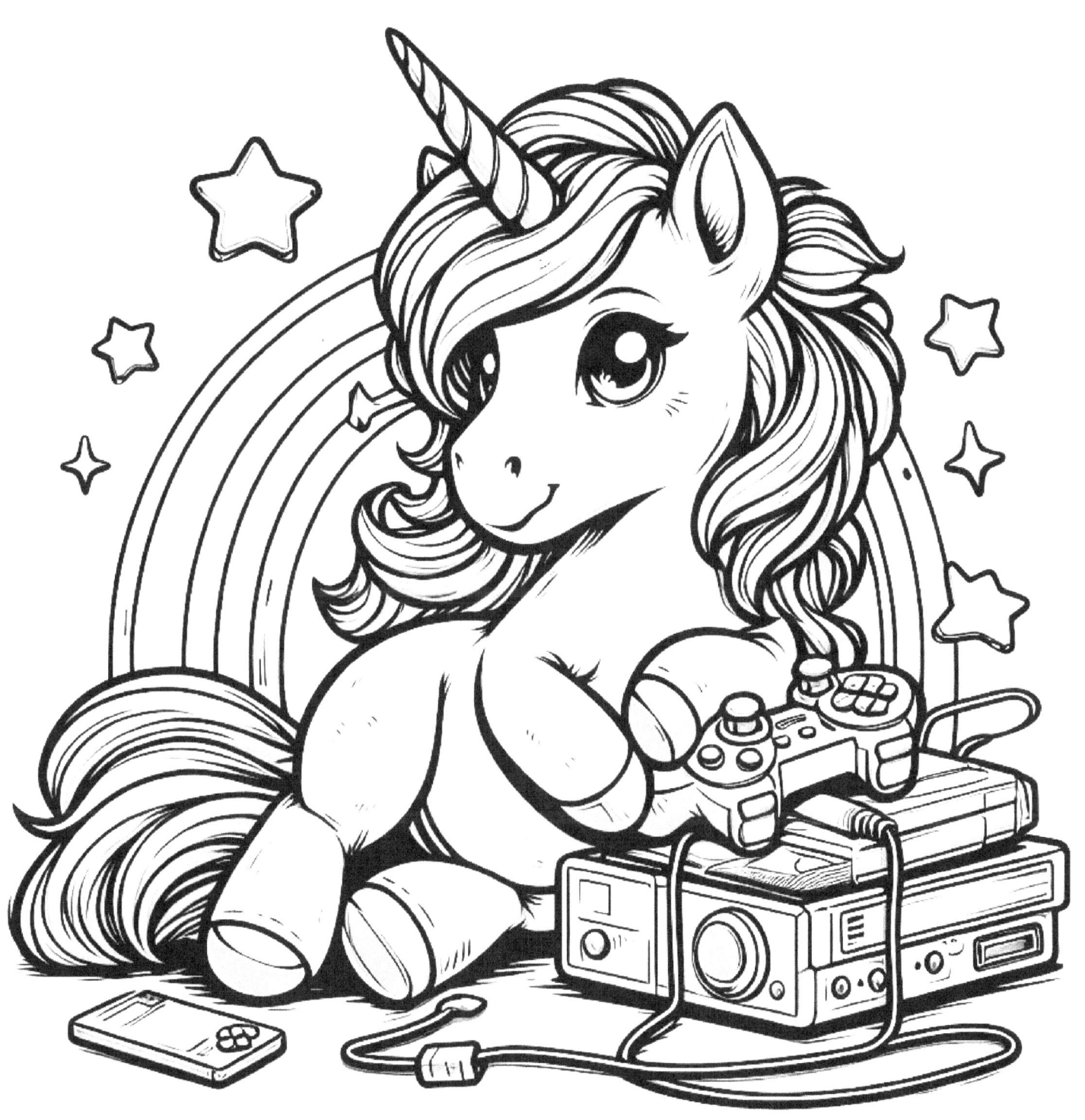

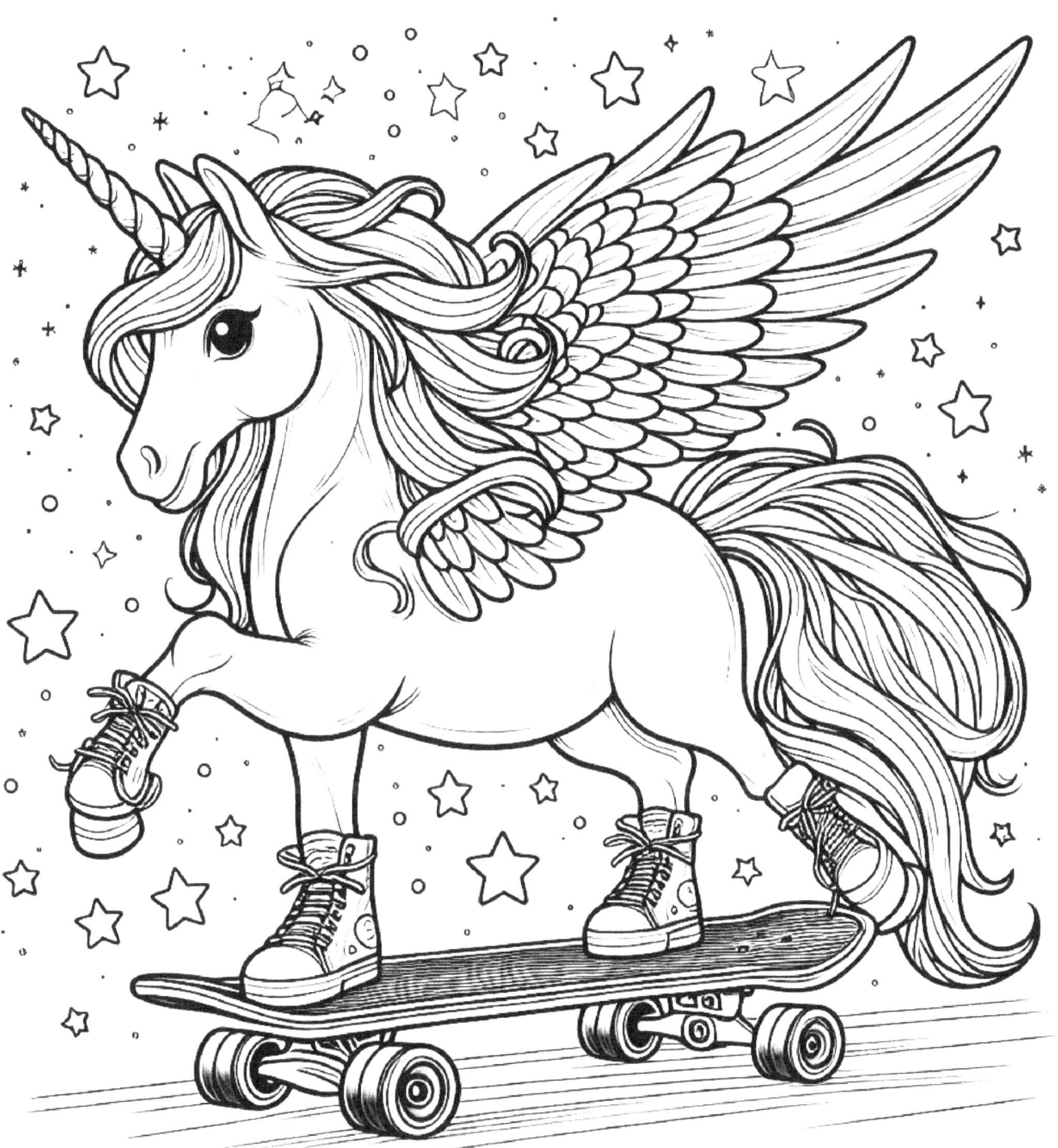

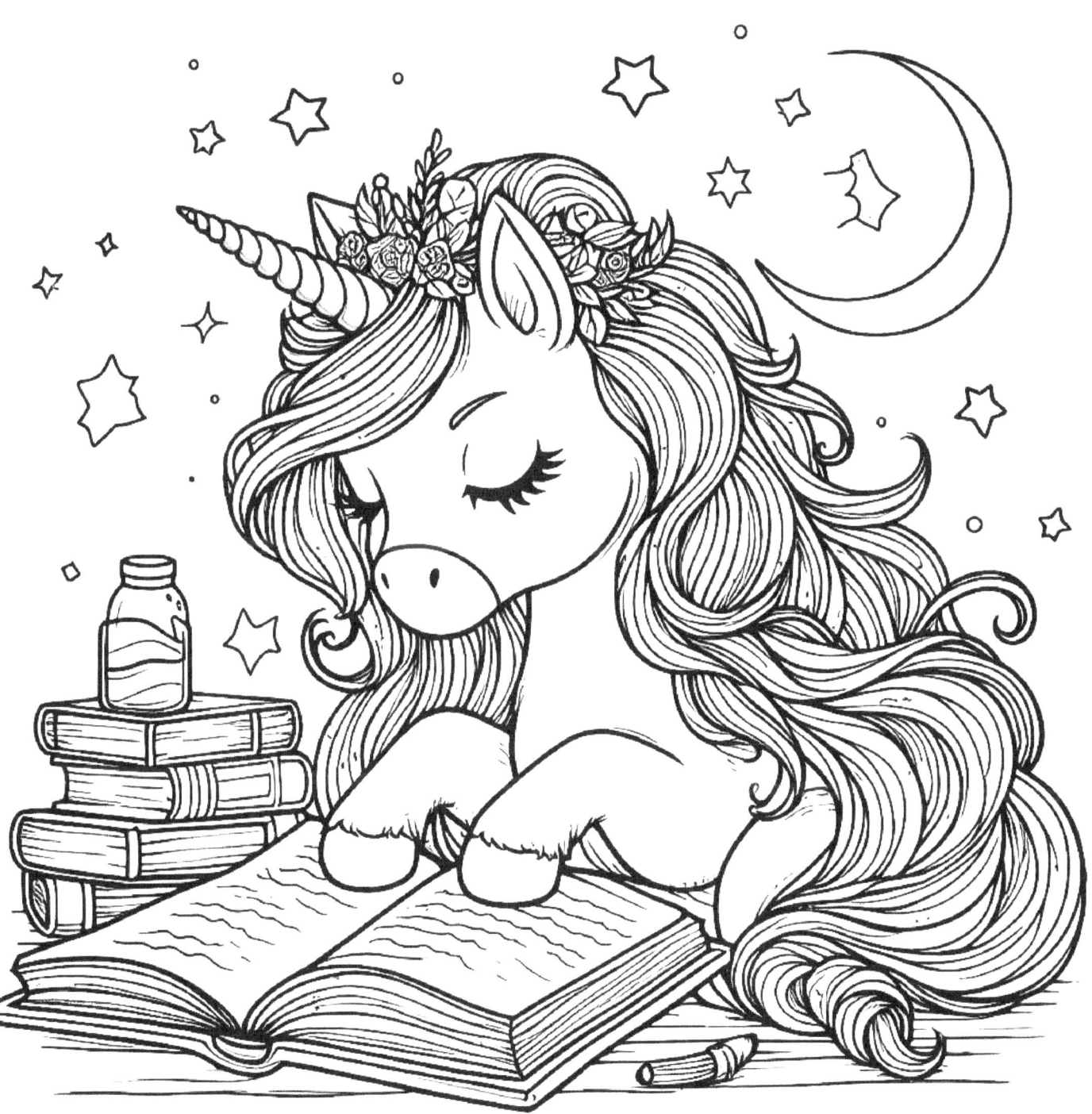

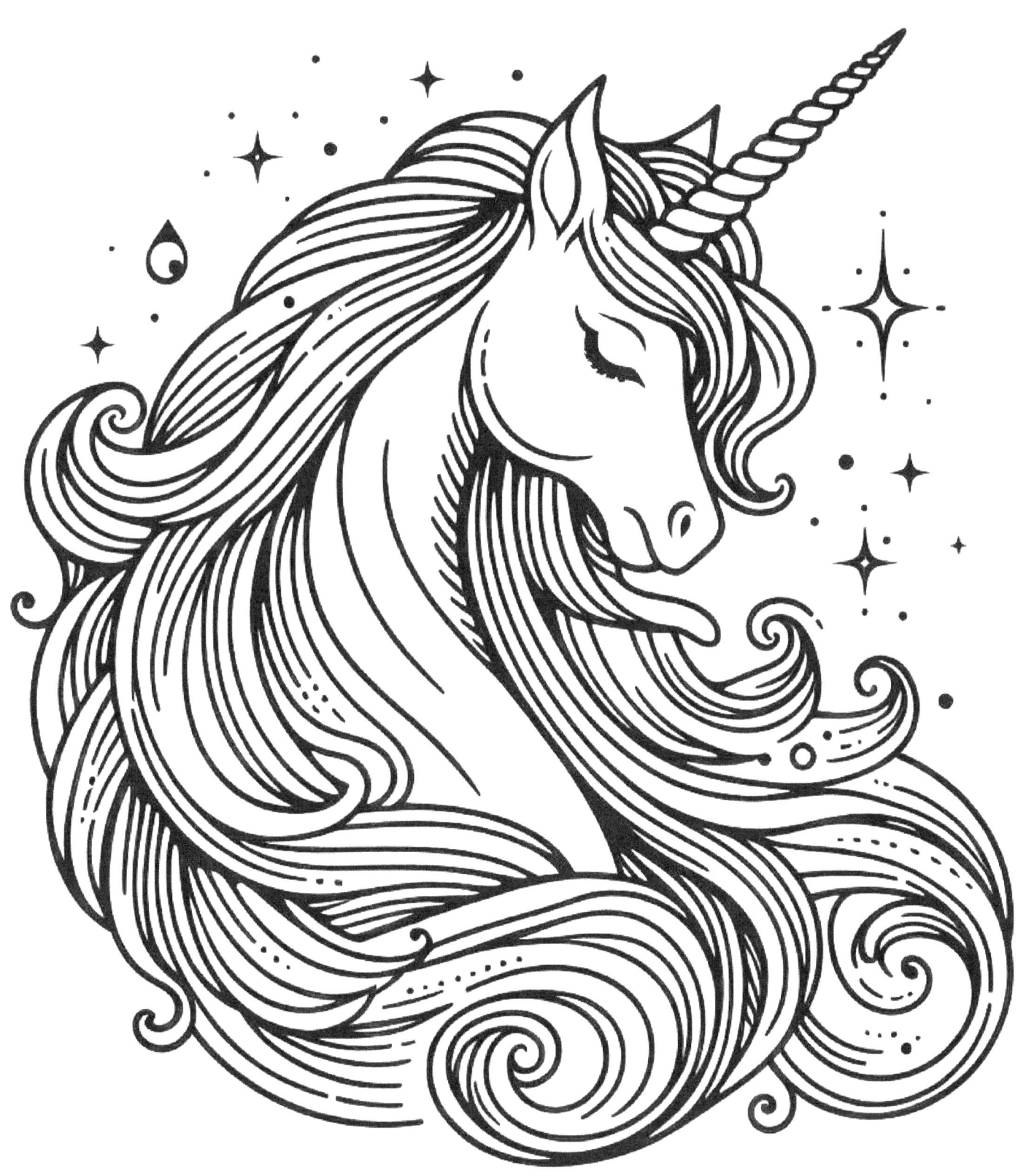

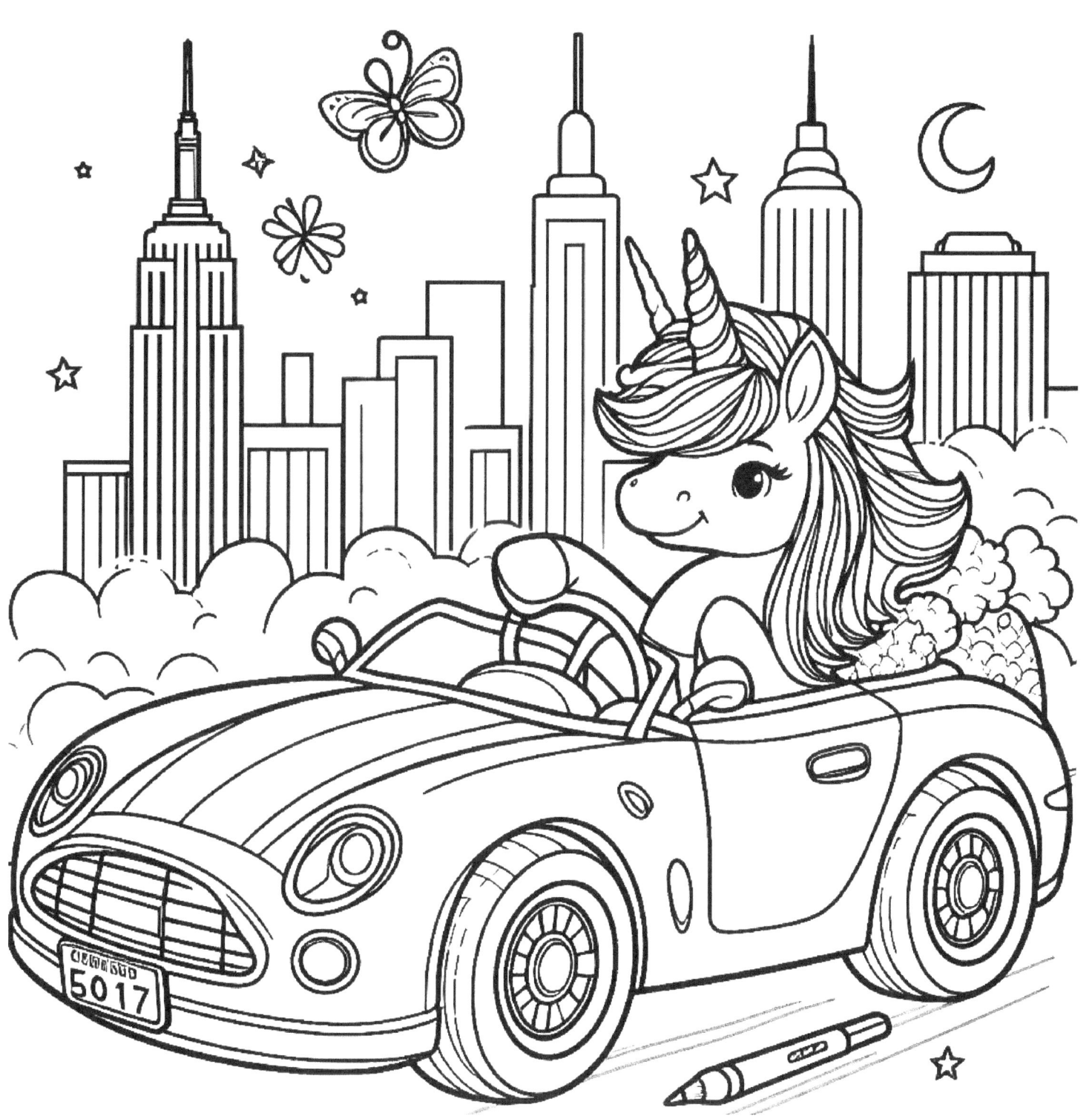

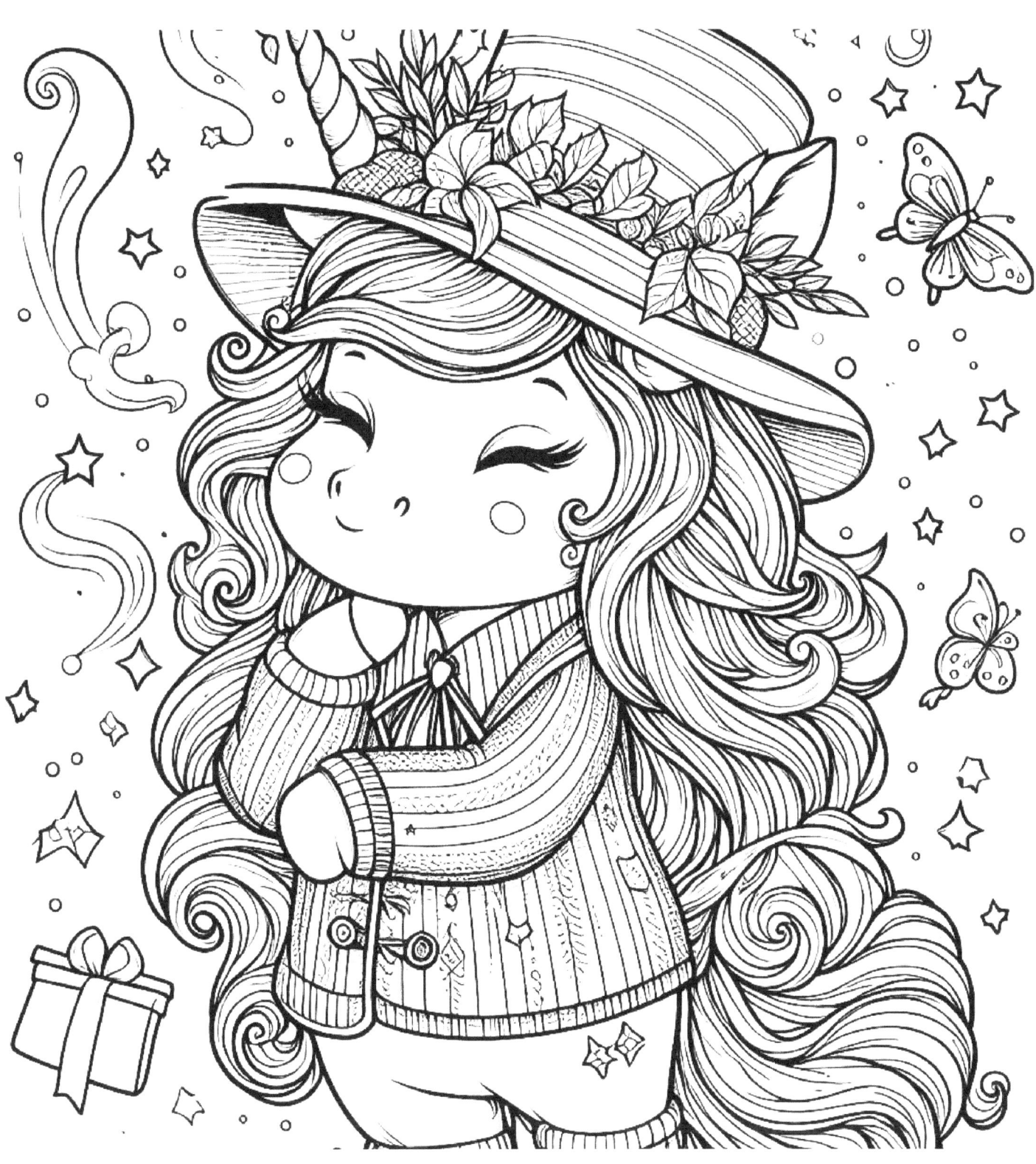

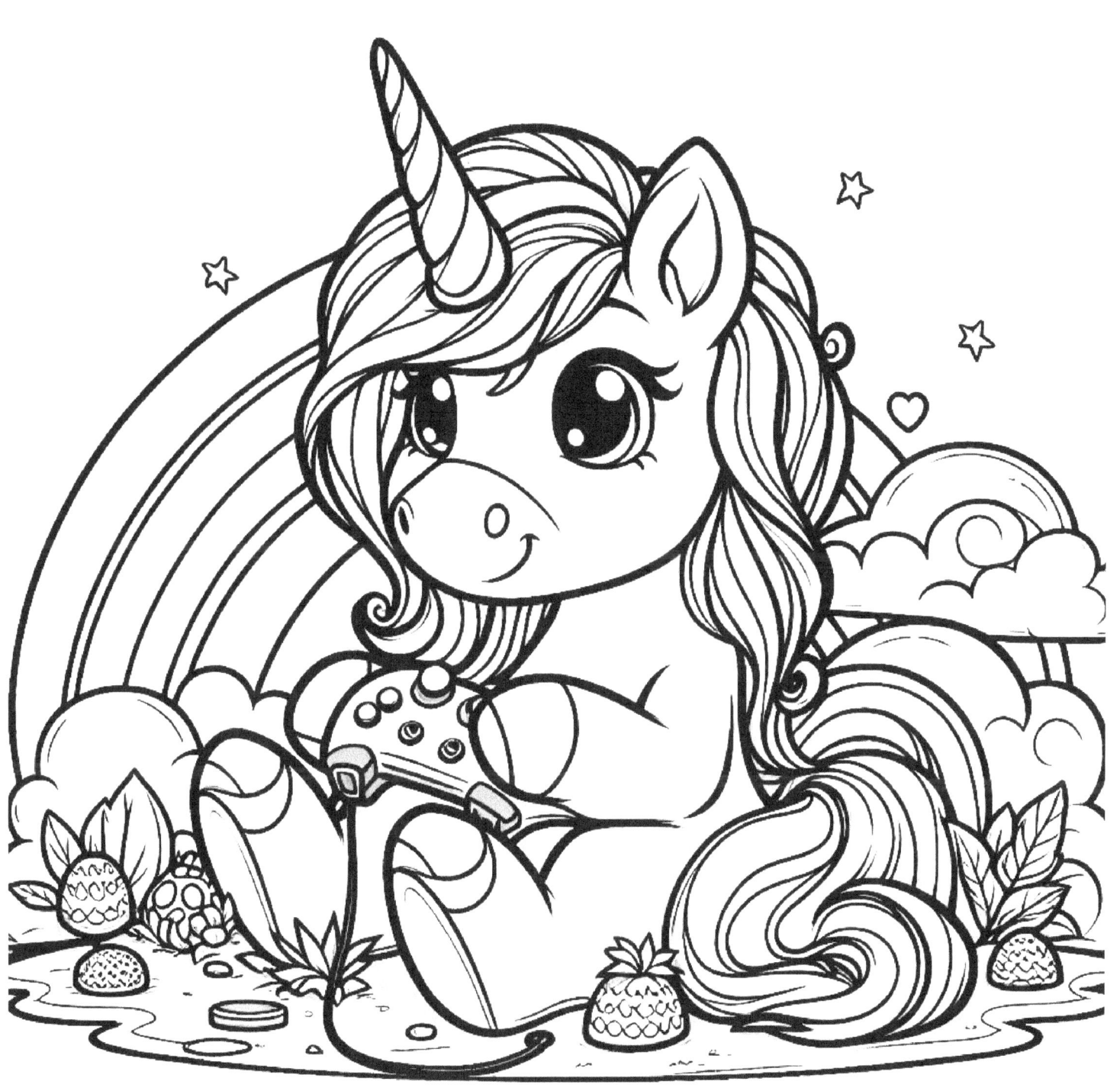

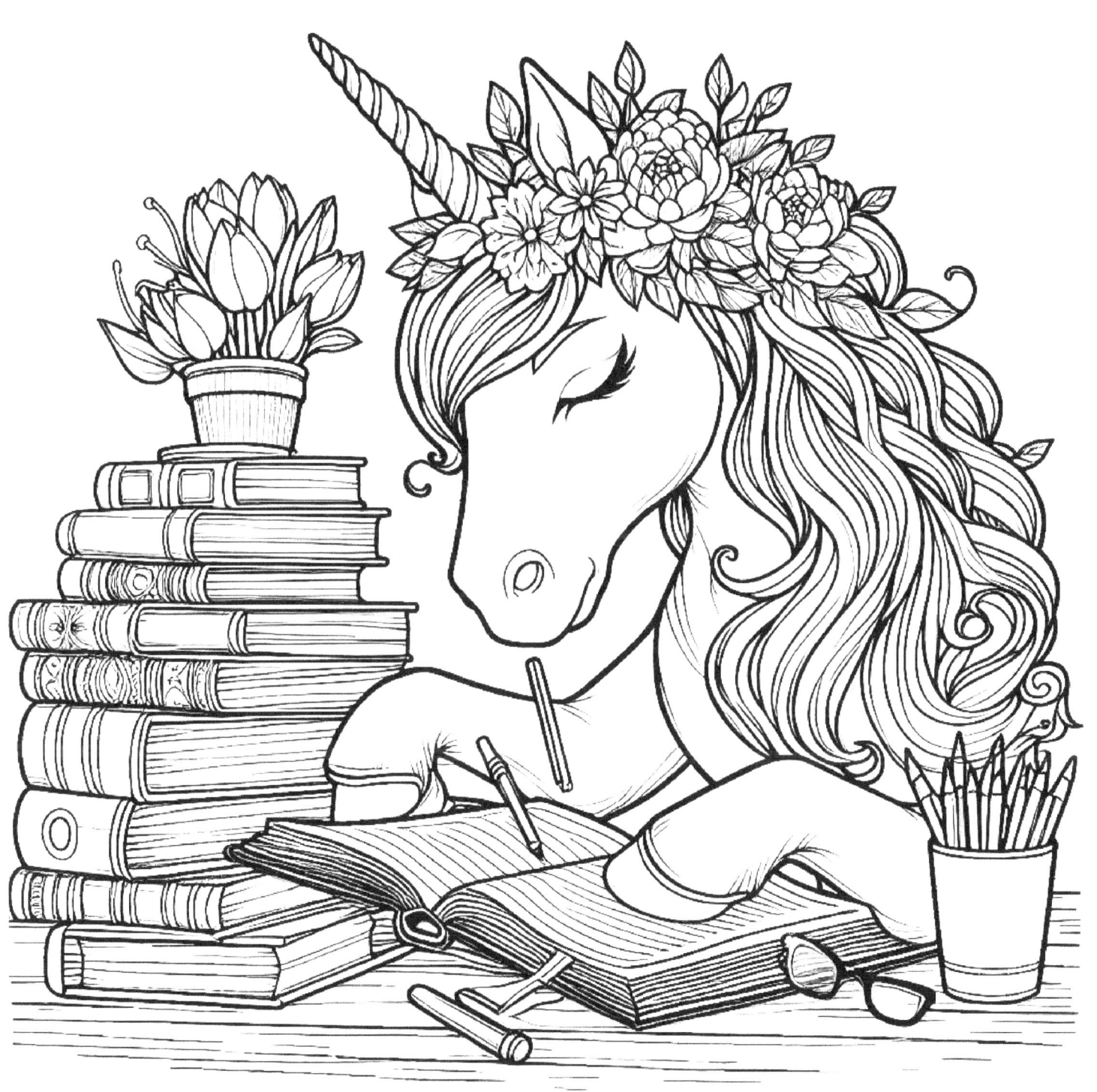

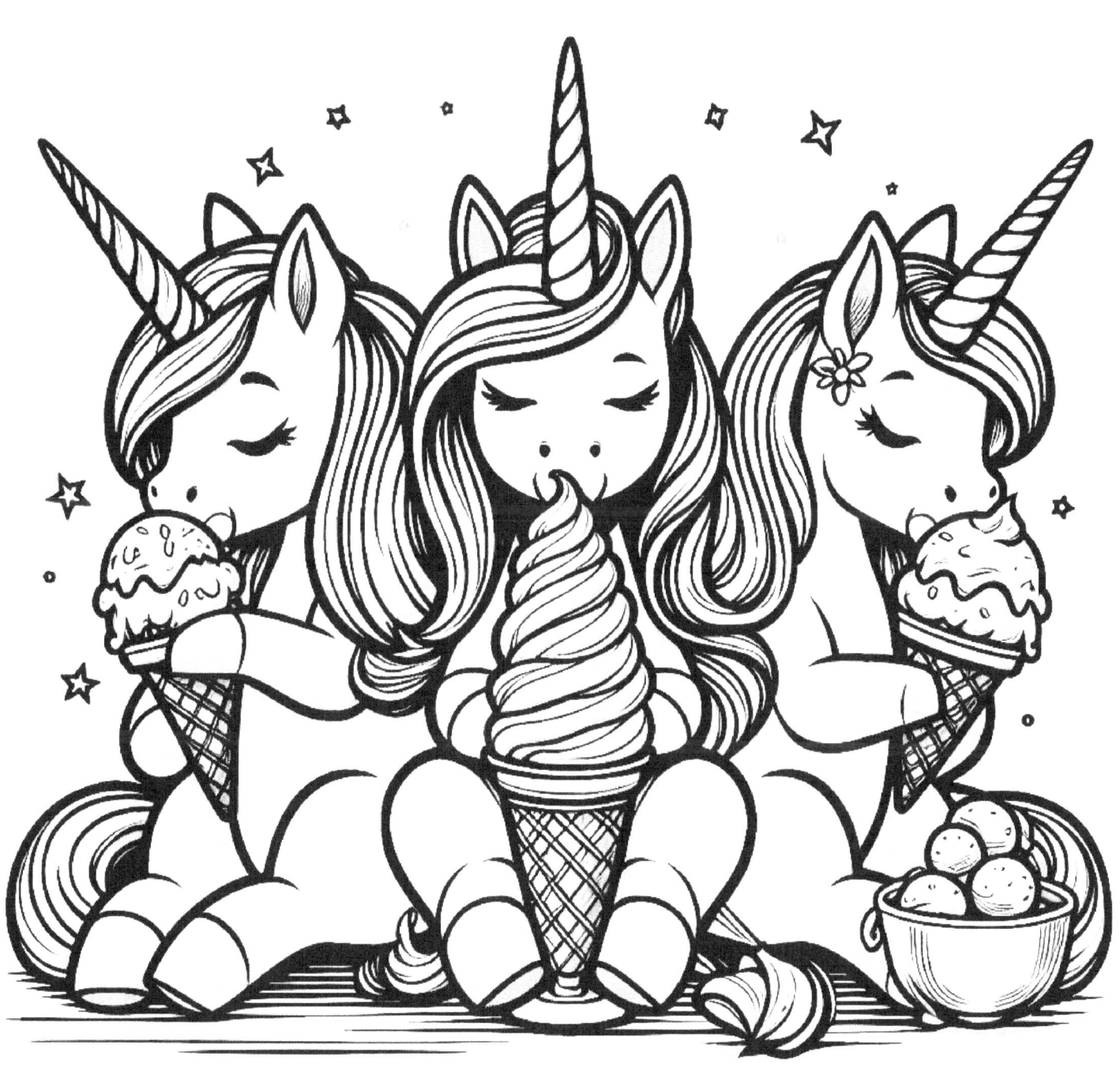

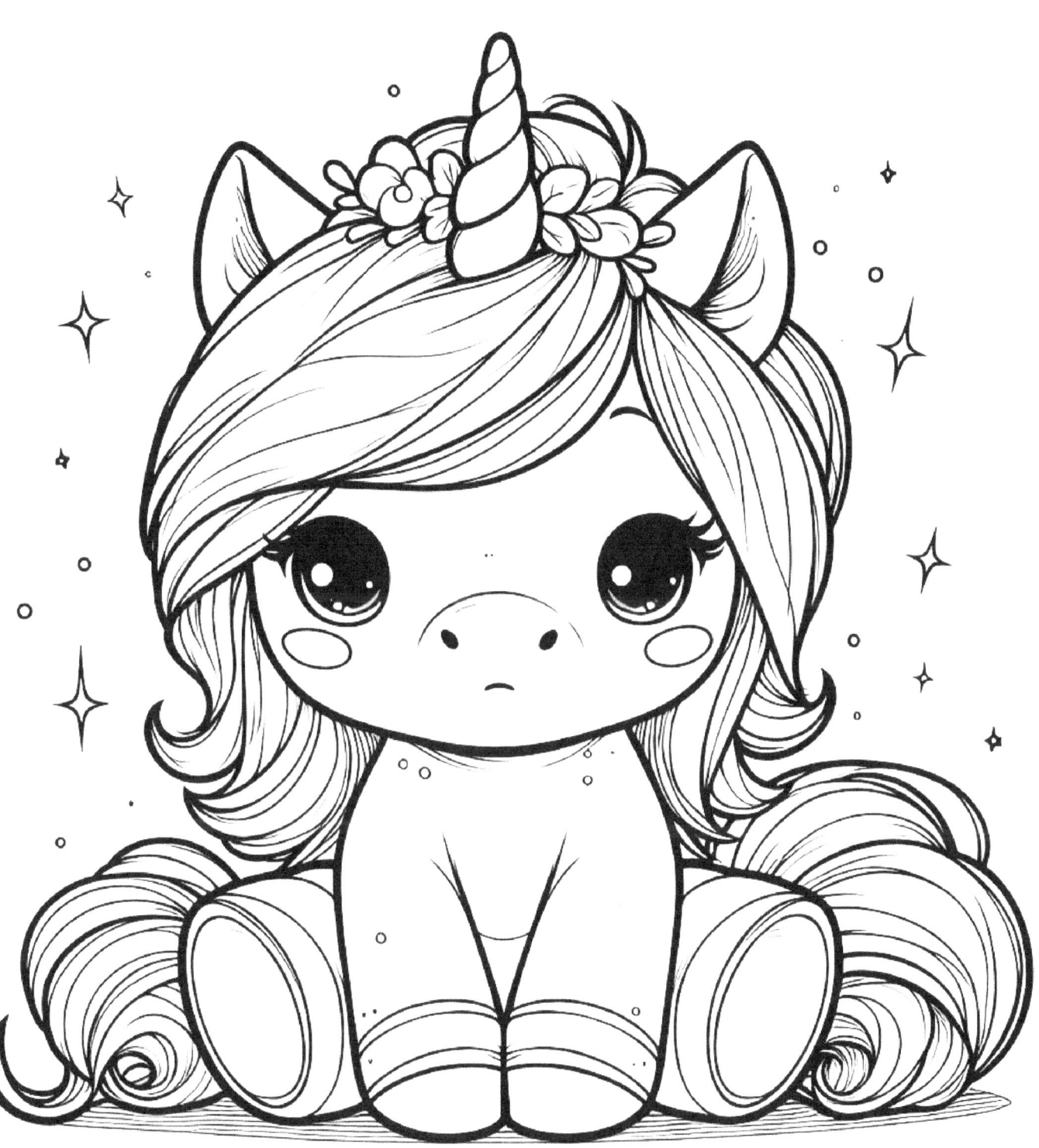

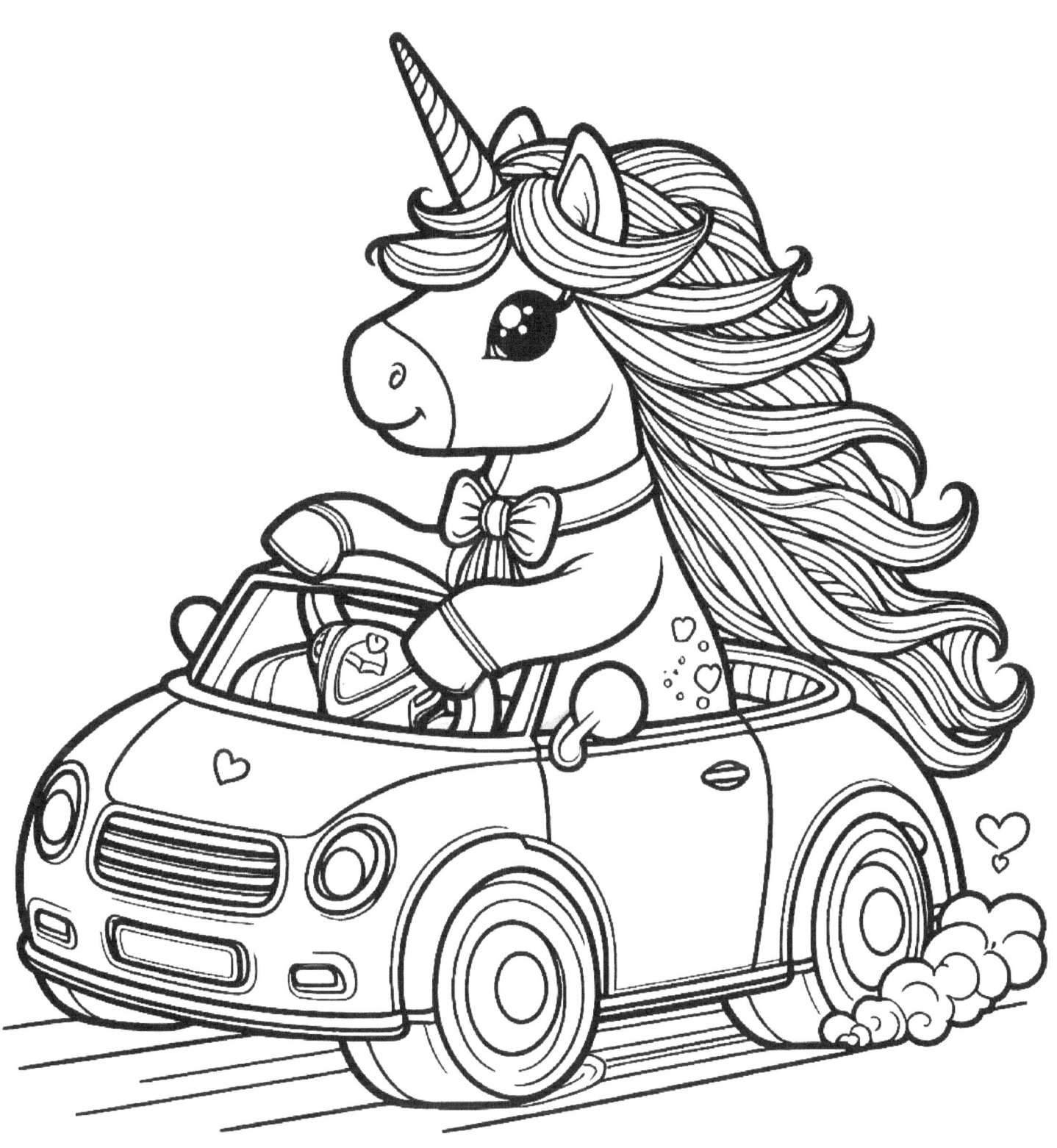

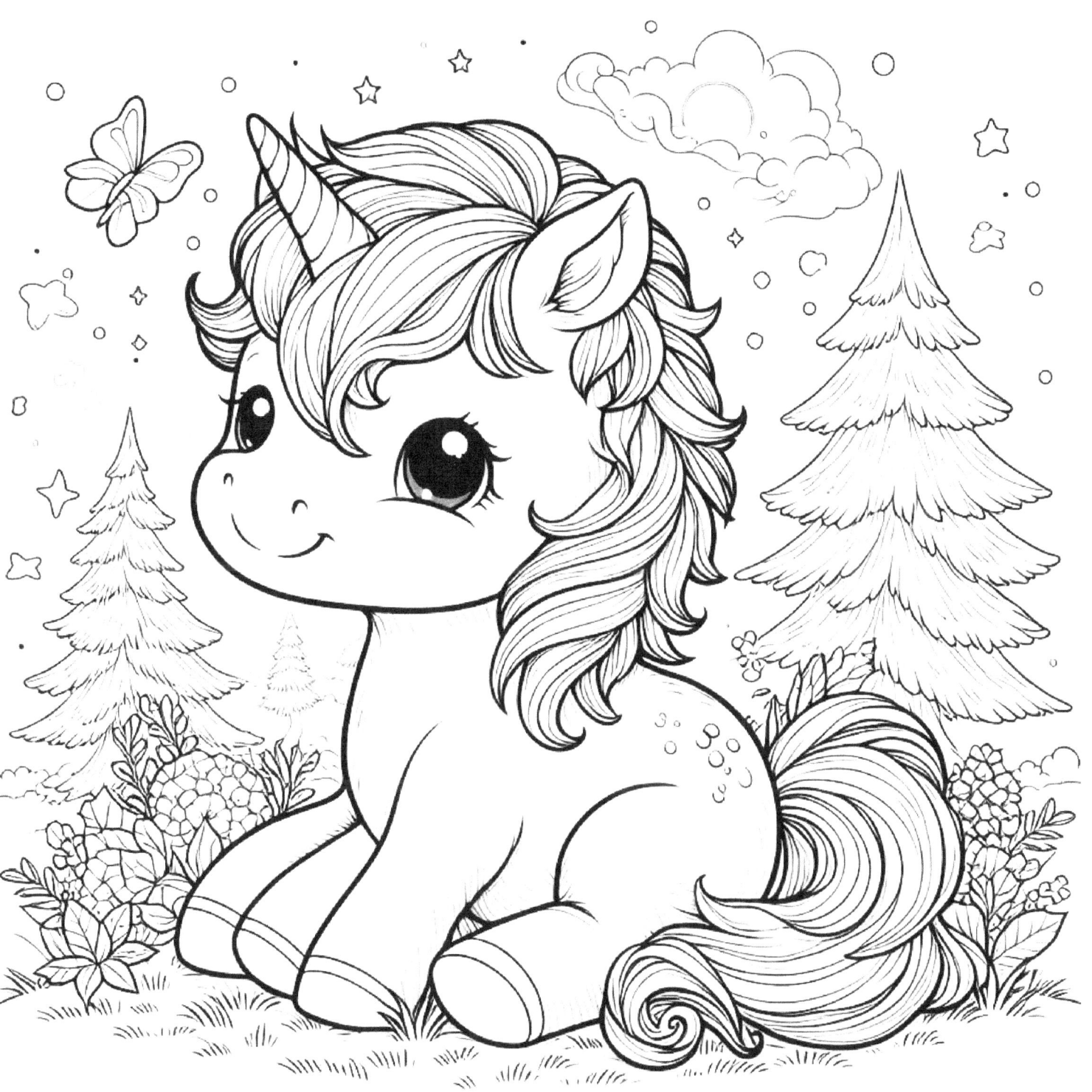

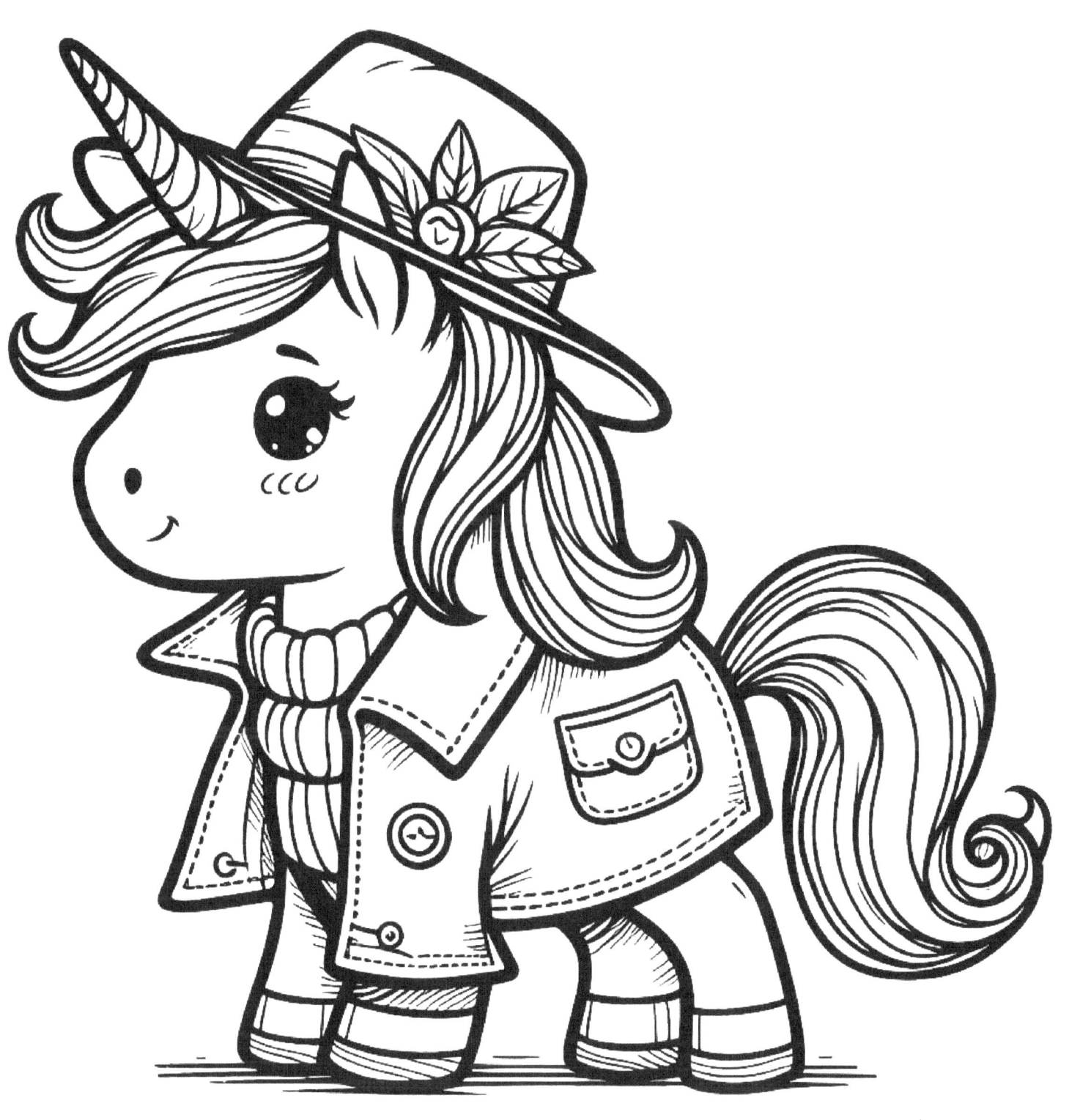

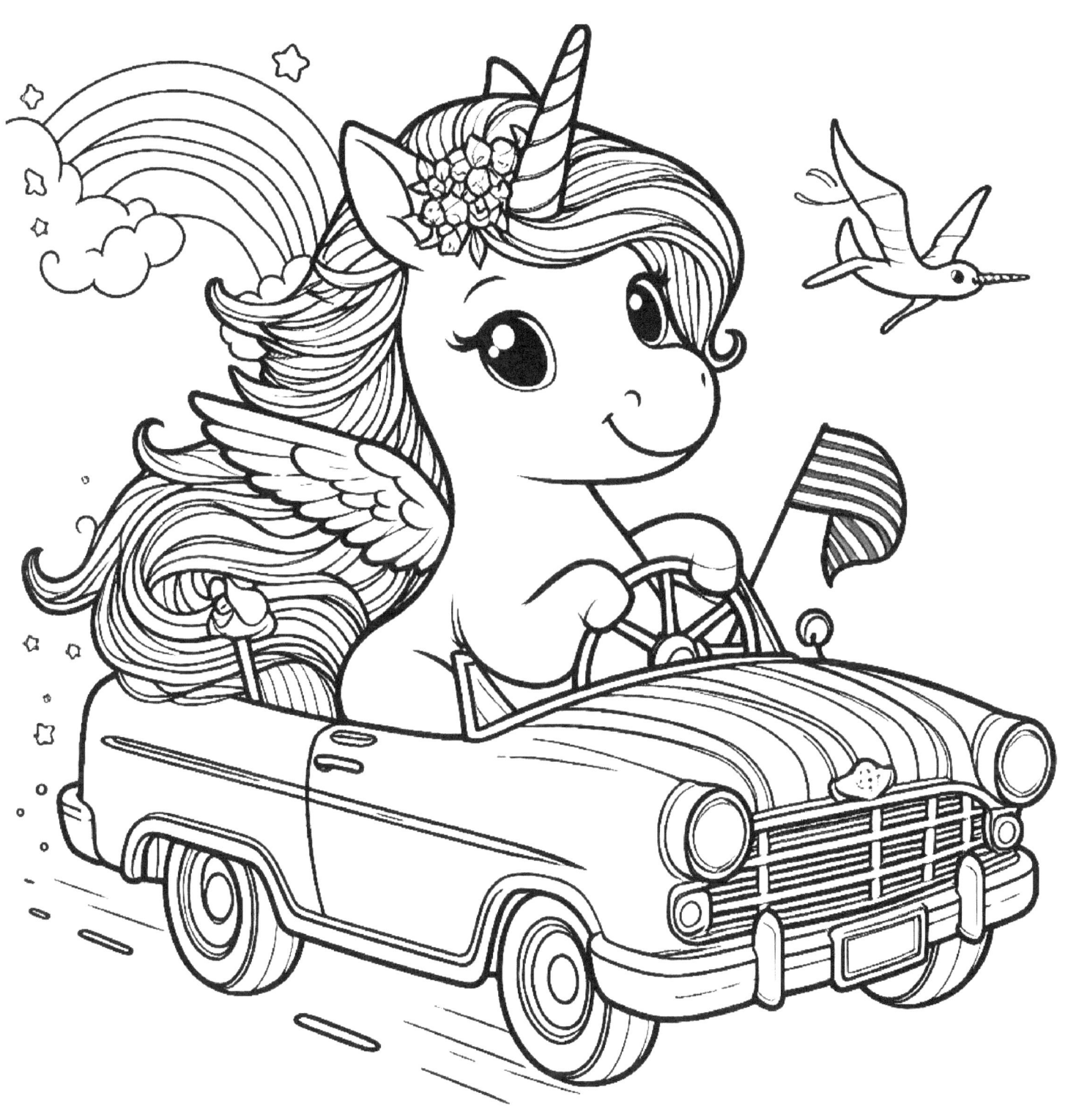

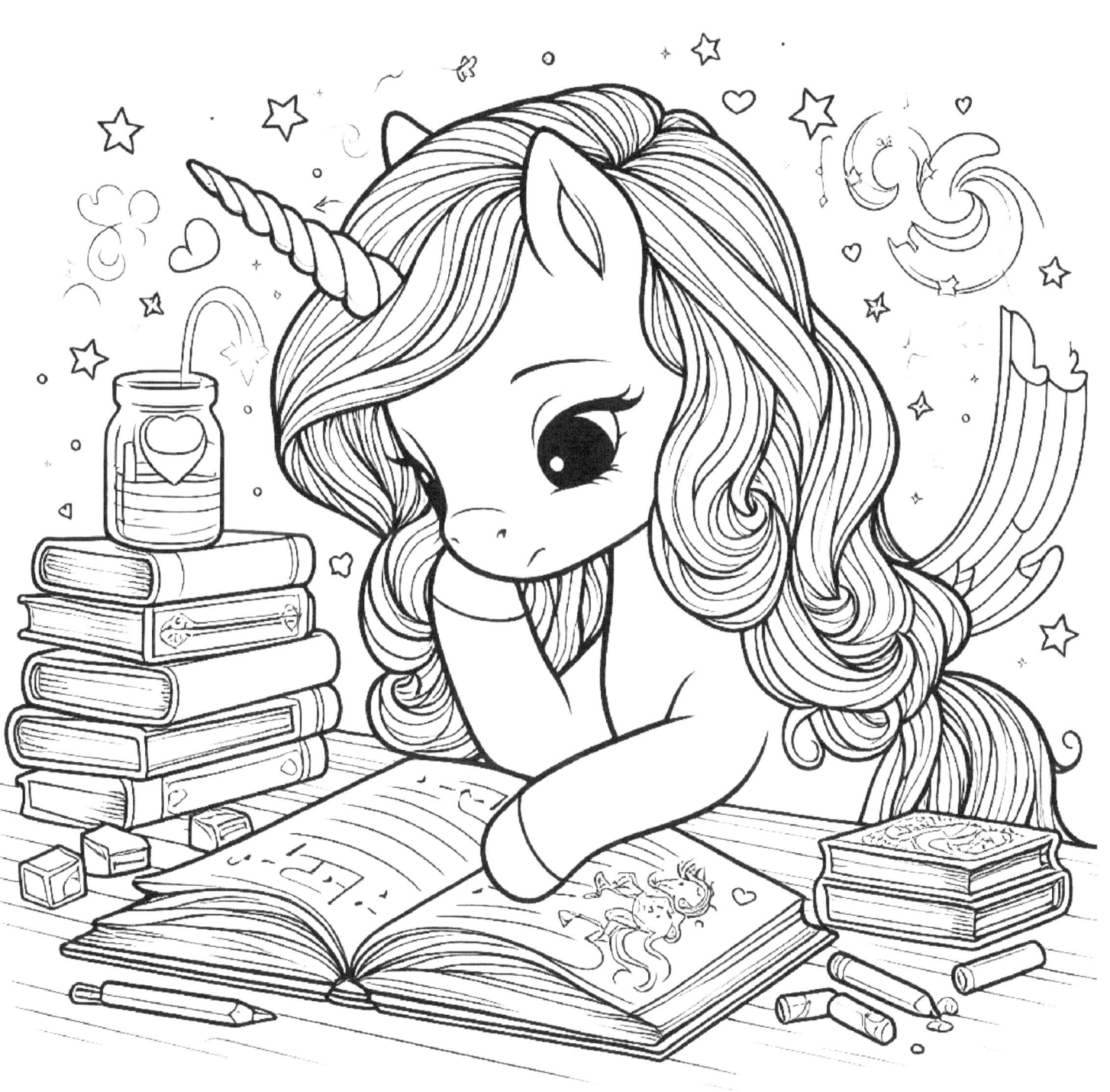

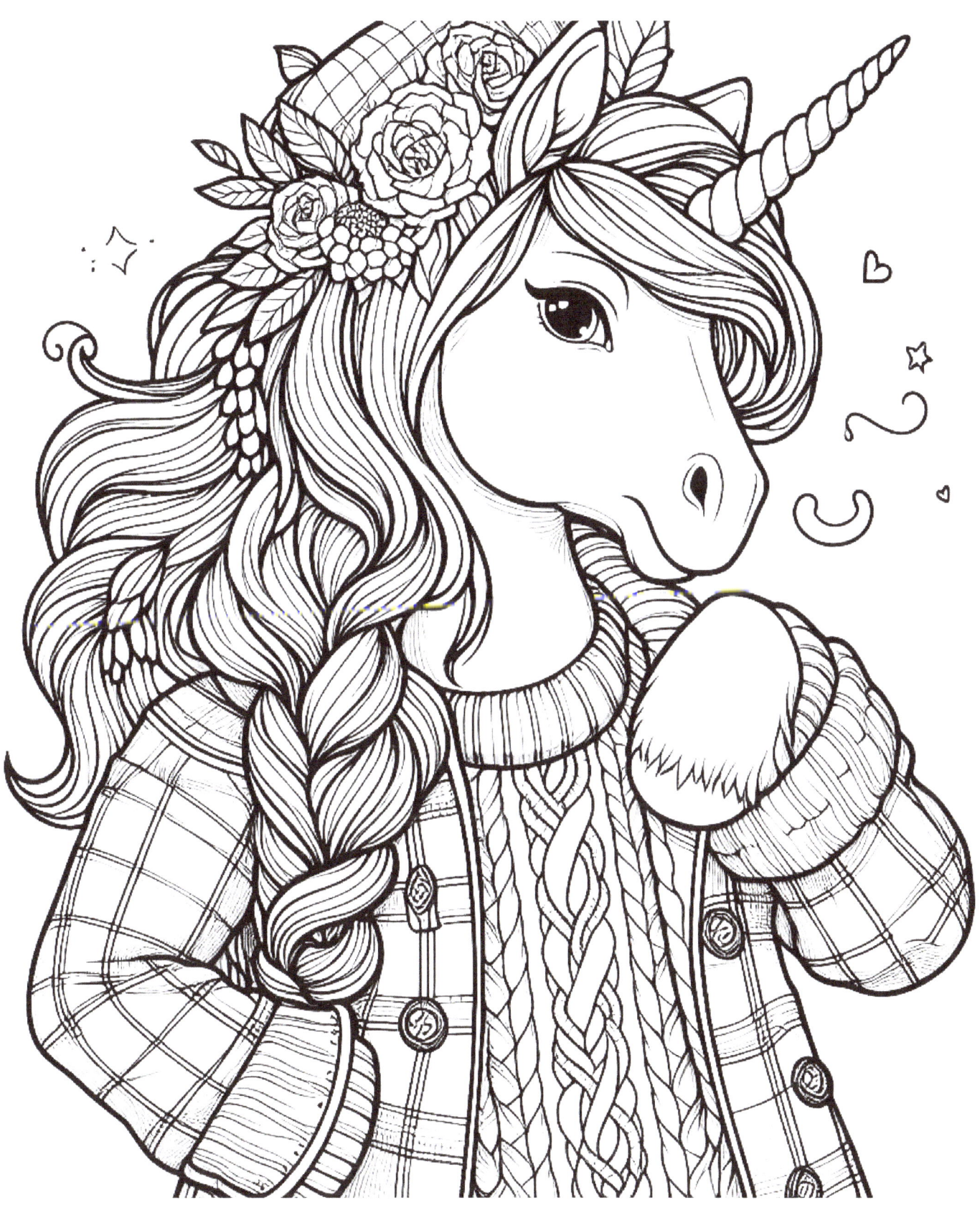

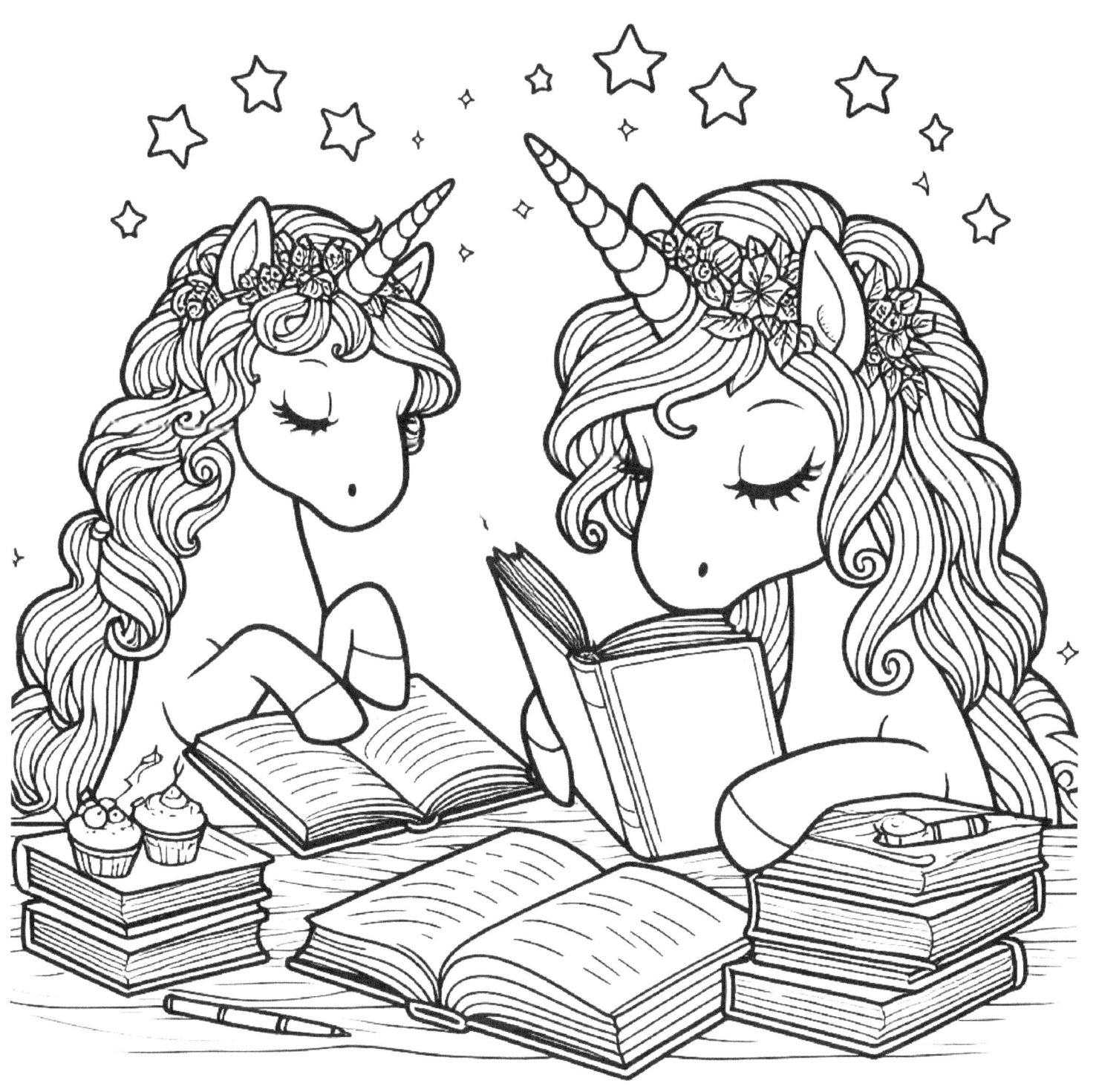

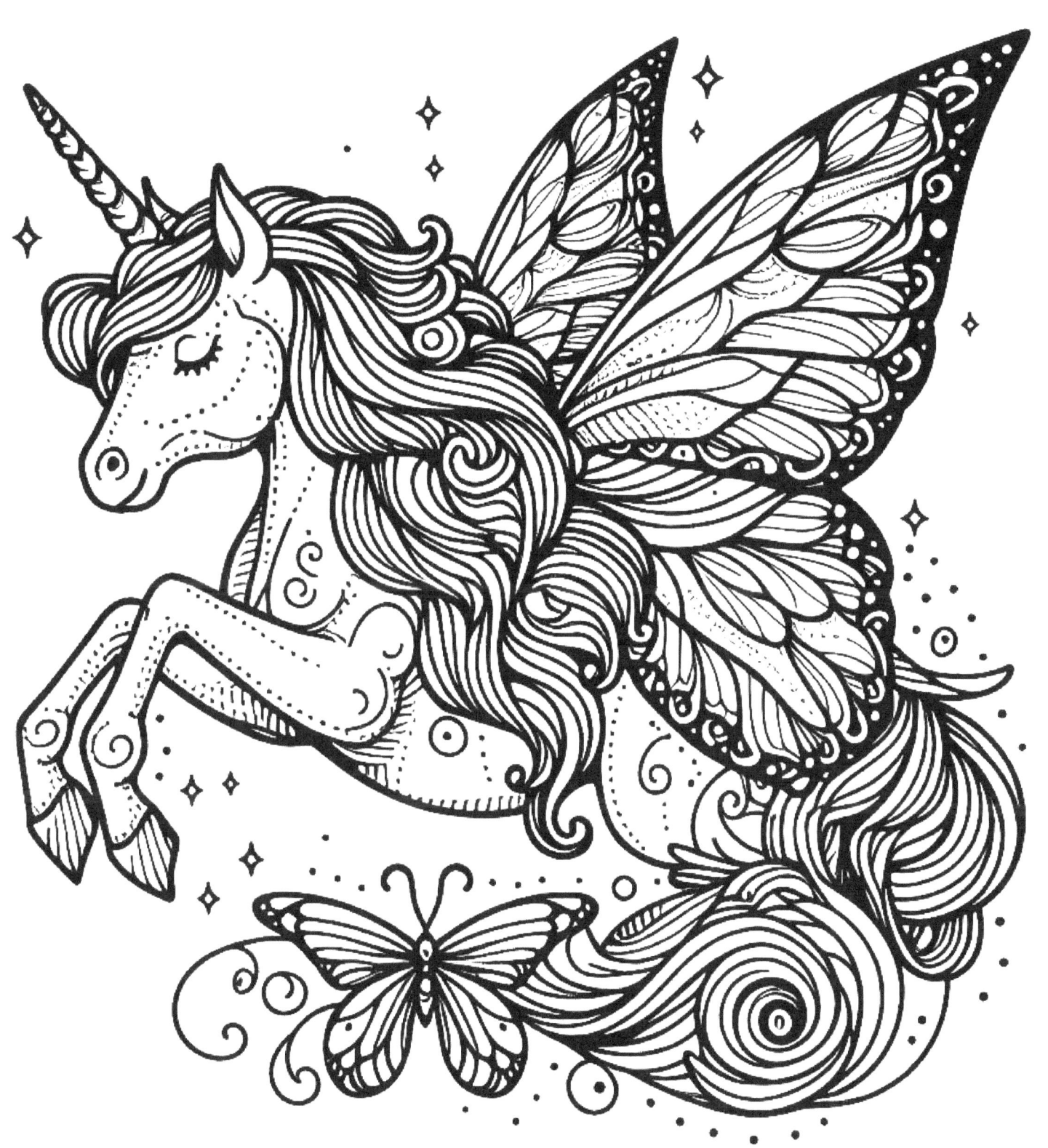

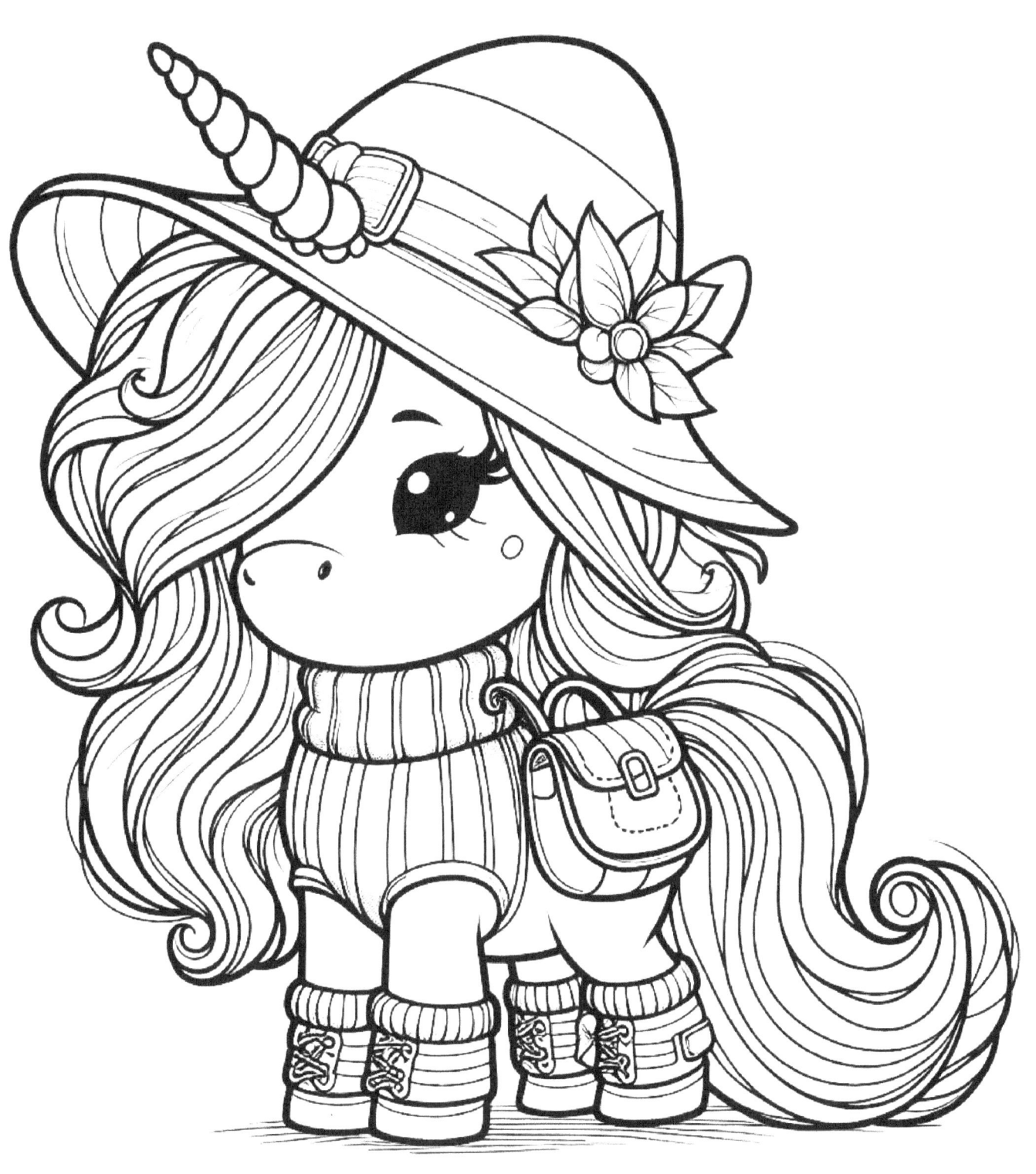

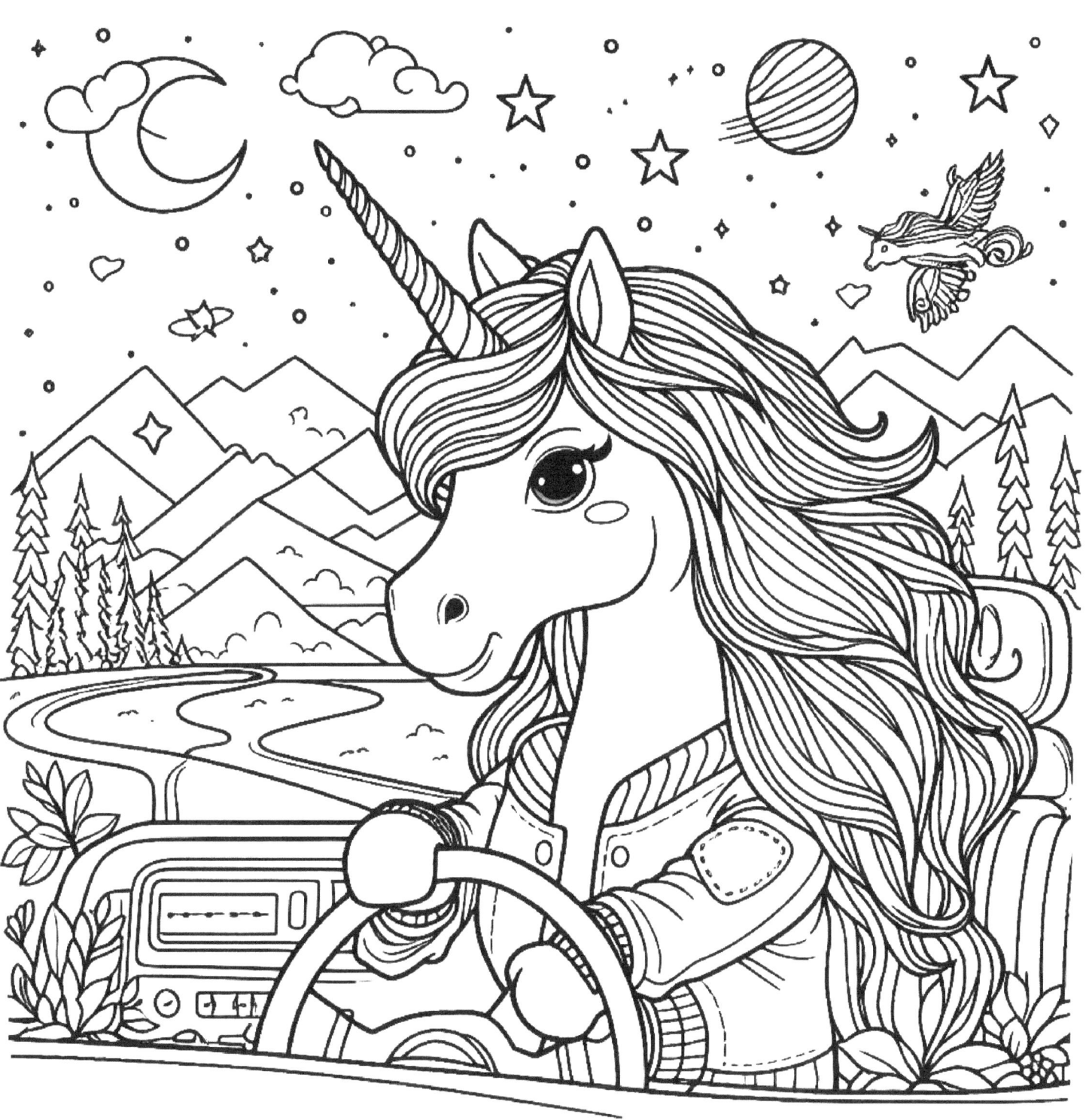

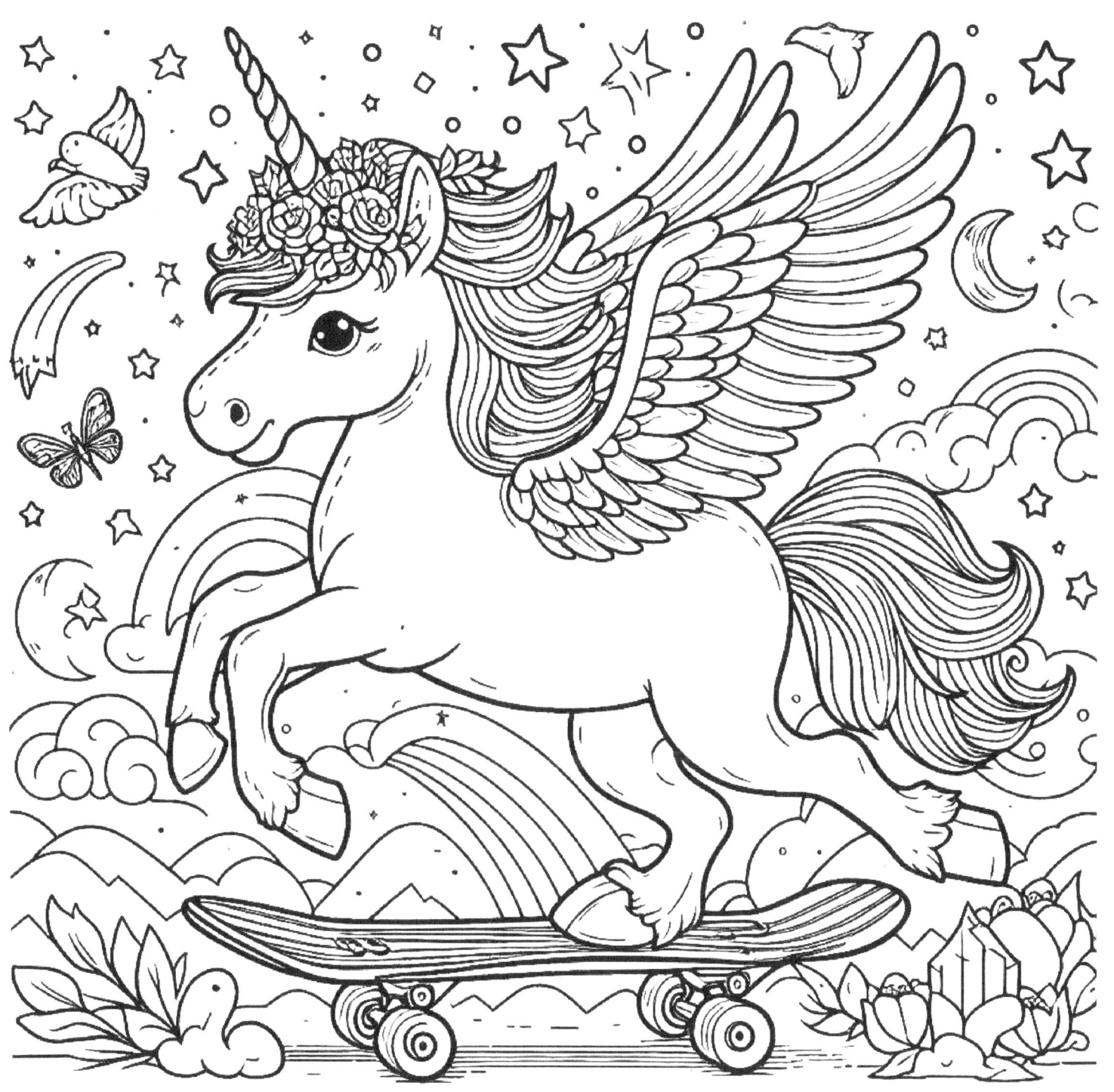

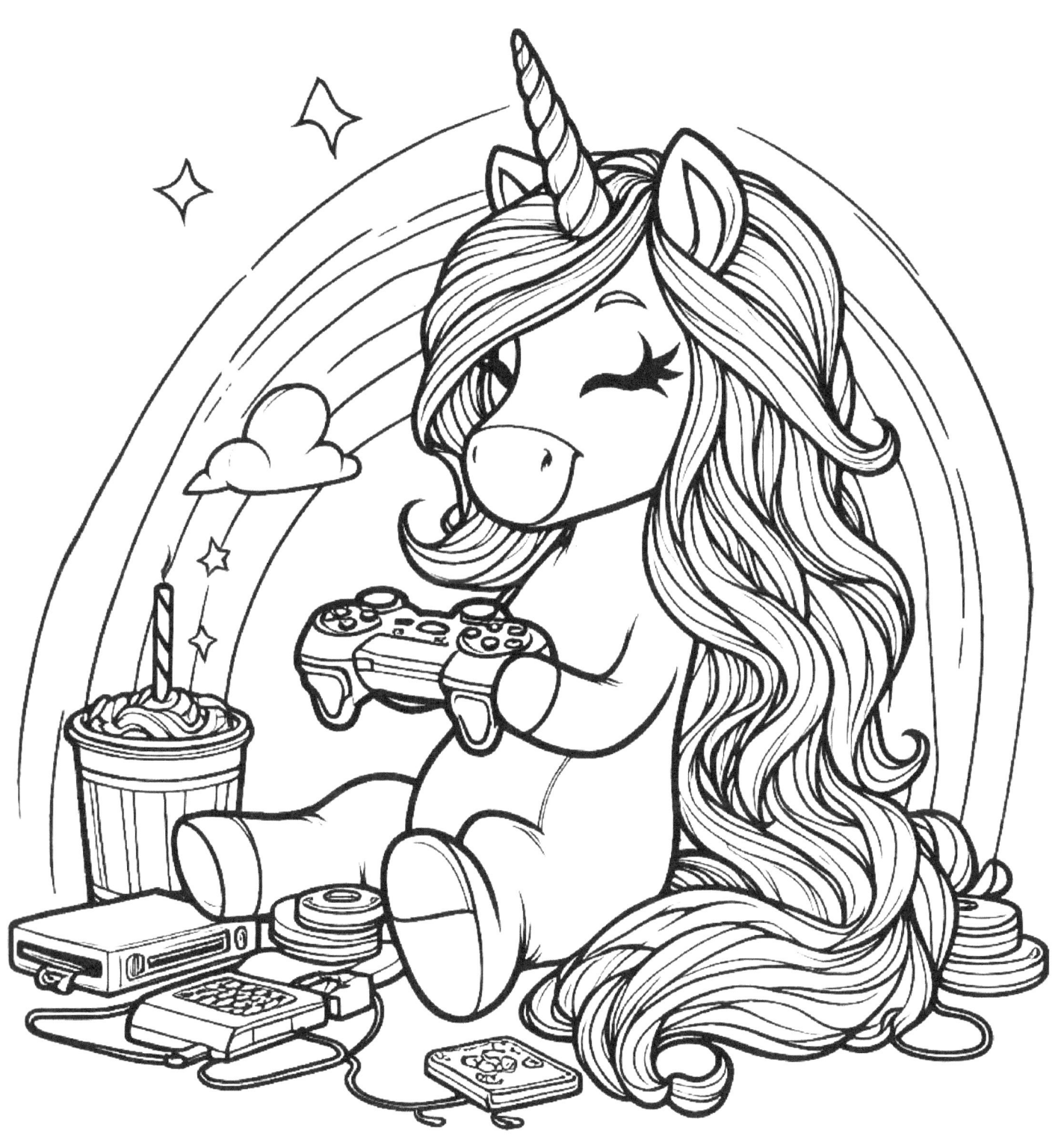

www.ingramcontent.com/pod-product-compliance
Lightning Source LLC
Chambersburg PA
CBHW062231220526

45471CB00009B/3432